Procedure and Documentation in Supply Chain Management

Business strategy books, Volume 1

SANJIVAN SAINI

Published by SANJIVAN SAINI, 2023.

PROCEDURE AND DOCUMENTATION IN SUPPLY CHAIN MANAGEMENT

First edition. October 7, 2023.

ISBN: 979-8223306290

Written by SANJIVAN SAINI.

In **"Procedure and Documentation in Supply Chain Management,"** author Sanjivan Saini provides a comprehensive guide to the intricacies of managing procedures and documentation in the dynamic field of supply chain management. This book delves into the critical aspects of logistics, documentation, and the various processes that underpin the movement of goods and materials across diverse industries. Saini offers valuable insights and practical knowledge for professionals, students, and anyone seeking a deeper understanding of supply chain operations. The book covers a wide range of topics, organized into several key sections:

Section 1: Logistics Management Process

- This section lays the foundation for understanding the logistics management process, covering topics such as the logistics process itself, the diverse industries engaged in logistics, the role of raw material suppliers, product manufacturing, transportation organizations, and the critical connection with marketplaces and customers.

Section 2: Warehousing and Documentation

- Here, the focus shifts to warehousing and the essential role it plays in supply chains. Saini explains the basis of documentation and emphasizes the importance of proper documentation practices in logistics. The section also delves into the various types of documents used and the circumstances in which they come into play.

Section 3: Raw Material Documents

- This section provides a detailed examination of the documents involved in the supply chain, from those required by raw material suppliers to documents necessary for product suppliers, transport organizations, and traders, both inland and overseas. It also touches on government processes, Chamber of Commerce requirements, and certificates of origin.

Section 4: Transport Documents

- Section 4 is a comprehensive exploration of documents required in transport, covering a wide array of topics including invoices, delivery challans, tax forms, waybills, bills of lading, and customs-related documents. The section also highlights aspects of rail and road transport, entry taxes, and transit passes.

Section 5: Documentation in the Organization

- The final section of the book delves into various documents and certificates used within organizations. Topics include maintenance certificates for trucks, warehousing safety, rail goods wagons, air cargo maintenance, and sea worthiness certificates for cargo ships. The section concludes with insights into cargo information documents, classification societies, stability booklets, and marine loss insurance claims.

Throughout the book, Sanjivan Saini emphasizes the importance of adhering to best practices in documentation, which are essential for efficiency, compliance, risk management, and transparency in supply chain operations. Readers will gain valuable knowledge about the critical role documentation plays in various aspects of logistics and supply chain management.

"Procedure and Documentation in Supply Chain Management" is a valuable resource that equips readers with the knowledge and tools needed to navigate the complexities of logistics and documentation in today's global supply chain landscape. Whether you are a logistics professional, student, or industry enthusiast, this book provides a comprehensive and practical guide to the subject.

TABLE OF CONTENT

CST forms
TIN services
Way bill
Bill of lading
Sea way bill
Customs Ice gate
Rail goods way bill
Entry tax form
Octroi forms
Transit pass
Packaging list
Log Book:
R.C. (Registration Certificate) Book:
Tax Paid Certificate:
Transport Permit:
Protection authentication
Nature of goods transported
Weight of Goods Information:
Container Safety Certificate:
Health Certificate:
Customs Clearing Certificate:
Warehousing Dues Paid Certificate:
Crew Qualification Certificate:
Insurance policy(E Insurance)
In bound consignment process, outbound consignment process
Goods and Services Tax (GST):
Documents relating to accidents and claims

Chapter-4 Documents for sea transport

Bill of lading, Types,
Crew passenger health certificate

Port Due
Light house due clearing certificate
Cargo information documents
Dutiable, Non dutiable list
Crew qualification certificate
List of life saving appliances certificate and Dry docking certificate
Classification societies certificate
Stability booklet
Certificate of inspection of goods
Documents for marine loss insurance claim.

Chapter-5 Documents with in the Organisation

Truck maintenance certificate

Warehousing safety certificate

Warehousing material handling equipment safety certificate

Rail goods wagon safety maintenance certificates

Air Cargo maintenance certificate

Cargo ships sea worthiness certificate

Staffs health regulation

Up keeping of premises certificate

Routine maintenance of building records and Dos and Donts while handling different documents.

Chapter-1 Logistics Management Process

Introduction

The logistics management process involves the planning, implementation, and control of the efficient flow and storage of goods, services, and information from the point of origin to the point of consumption. It plays a crucial role in ensuring that products are delivered to customers in a timely and cost-effective manner. Here is an overview of the key steps in the logistics management process:

1. **Demand Forecasting:** The process begins with estimating future demand for products or services. Accurate forecasting helps in planning inventory levels and transportation requirements.
2. **Order Processing:** Once customer orders are received, they need to be processed efficiently. This includes order verification, payment processing, and order entry.
3. **Inventory Management:** Managing inventory levels is crucial to avoid overstocking or understocking. The goal is to have the right amount of stock to meet customer demand while minimizing carrying costs.
4. **Warehousing:** Goods are often stored in warehouses or distribution centers before being shipped to customers. Proper warehouse management ensures goods are stored safely and can be retrieved quickly when needed.
5. **Transportation Planning:** Selecting the most suitable mode of transportation (e.g., truck, ship, rail, air) and routing for shipping products to customers. This step involves optimizing routes for efficiency and cost-effectiveness.
6. **Order Picking and Packing:** Items are picked from inventory and packed for shipment. This includes ensuring proper

packaging to prevent damage during transit.

7. **Shipping:** Goods are transported to their destination using the chosen transportation method. Tracking and monitoring shipments is important to ensure timely delivery.
8. **Receiving and Unloading:** When goods arrive at their destination, they must be received and unloaded efficiently. This step involves inspecting incoming shipments for accuracy and quality.
9. **Distribution:** Products may go through additional distribution channels, such as wholesalers or retailers, before reaching the end customer.
10. **Information Management:** Throughout the logistics process, information about orders, shipments, and inventory levels is crucial. Advanced technologies like RFID and ERP systems are often used to track and manage this information.
11. **Performance Measurement:** Key performance indicators (KPIs) are used to measure the effectiveness of the logistics process. Metrics such as on-time delivery, inventory turnover, and cost per unit shipped help identify areas for improvement.
12. **Continuous Improvement:** Based on performance data and feedback, logistics processes are continually reviewed and optimized to reduce costs, enhance efficiency, and improve customer satisfaction.

Effective logistics management is essential for businesses to meet customer expectations, minimize costs, and remain competitive in today's global marketplace. It requires a combination of strategic planning, technology utilization, and operational excellence to ensure the smooth flow of goods and information throughout the supply chain.

Types of industries engaged in logistics

process

The logistics process is a critical component of various industries, as it involves the efficient movement and management of goods and information across the supply chain. Here are some of the types of industries that heavily rely on logistics:

1. **Retail:** Retail businesses, including brick-and-mortar stores and e-commerce companies, depend on logistics to ensure products are delivered to customers on time. Inventory management, warehousing, and last-mile delivery are essential in this industry.
2. **Manufacturing:** Manufacturers require logistics to transport raw materials to their facilities, manage production processes, and distribute finished products to customers. Efficient logistics are vital for maintaining production schedules and meeting customer demands.
3. **Automotive:** The automotive industry involves complex supply chains with multiple components and assembly processes. Logistics are crucial for sourcing parts, managing assembly lines, and delivering vehicles to dealerships.
4. **Agriculture and Food:** This industry relies on logistics for the timely transport of perishable goods like fruits, vegetables, and dairy products. Cold chain logistics, which maintains temperature-controlled conditions, is particularly important in this sector.
5. **Pharmaceuticals and Healthcare:** Pharmaceuticals and medical equipment must be handled with precision and care. Logistics ensure that medicines, vaccines, and medical supplies are distributed safely and securely to hospitals, pharmacies, and clinics.
6. **Technology and Electronics:** Electronics manufacturers require efficient logistics for sourcing components, assembling

products, and delivering them to global markets. Supply chain management is critical to meet consumer demand for devices and gadgets.

7. **Energy and Oil:** The energy sector relies on logistics for the transportation of fuels, oil, and gas. Supply chain management in this industry ensures a steady and reliable supply of energy resources.
8. **Construction:** The construction industry requires logistics for the transportation of building materials, heavy equipment, and machinery to construction sites. Efficient logistics help keep construction projects on schedule and within budget.
9. **Chemicals and Pharmaceuticals:** Chemical companies need logistics to manage the transportation and distribution of chemicals, including hazardous materials. Safety and compliance are top priorities in this sector.
10. **Textiles and Apparel:** The fashion industry relies on logistics for sourcing textiles, managing production processes, and distributing clothing and accessories to retail outlets around the world.
11. **Aerospace:** Aerospace manufacturers require precise logistics to source aerospace components, assemble aircraft, and deliver them to customers, including airlines and defense agencies.
12. **E-commerce and Logistics Services:** Logistics companies themselves form an industry dedicated to providing transportation, warehousing, and supply chain management services to various businesses. This sector has grown significantly with the rise of e-commerce.
13. **Consumer Goods:** This includes a wide range of products such as household goods, personal care items, and appliances. Logistics are essential for the distribution of these goods to retailers and consumers.

These industries represent just a few examples of those that rely on logistics processes to ensure the efficient flow of goods and information throughout their supply chains. Effective logistics management is crucial for businesses in these sectors to remain competitive and meet customer demands.

Supplier of raw materials

Suppliers of raw materials are businesses or entities that provide the necessary inputs or unprocessed materials needed for the production of goods or services in various industries. These raw materials can vary significantly depending on the industry and may include natural resources, components, or materials used in manufacturing processes. Here are some common types of suppliers of raw materials:

1. **Primary Resource Suppliers:** These suppliers provide natural resources like minerals, metals, agricultural products, and forestry products. For example, mining companies supply raw metals like iron ore or copper, while farms supply raw agricultural products such as wheat or cotton.
2. **Manufacturers of Components:** Many industries rely on suppliers who manufacture specific components or parts used in the production process. For instance, in the automotive industry, suppliers provide components like engines, tires, and electronic systems.
3. **Chemical Suppliers:** Chemical manufacturers supply raw materials such as chemicals, polymers, and specialty materials used in various sectors, including pharmaceuticals, plastics, and chemical processing.
4. **Textile Suppliers:** The textile industry depends on suppliers of raw materials like cotton, wool, synthetic fibers, and dyes for producing fabrics and clothing.
5. **Lumber and Timber Suppliers:** The construction and

woodworking industries rely on suppliers of raw timber and lumber for making furniture, building structures, and more.

6. **Energy Suppliers:** Industries like power generation and manufacturing often require raw materials like coal, natural gas, and oil to fuel their operations.
7. **Food Ingredient Suppliers:** The food and beverage industry depends on suppliers of raw ingredients such as grains, spices, sugar, and additives to produce various food products.
8. **Plastic Resin Suppliers:** Companies involved in plastics manufacturing rely on suppliers of plastic resins, which are the raw materials used to create plastic products.
9. **Paper and Pulp Suppliers:** The paper and packaging industry relies on suppliers of raw materials like wood pulp, paperboard, and specialty paper products.
10. **Electronics Component Suppliers:** Manufacturers of electronic devices rely on suppliers of raw materials like semiconductors, integrated circuits, and electronic components.
11. **Mining Companies:** These companies extract and supply raw materials like coal, metals, and minerals used in various industries, including construction, energy, and manufacturing.
12. **Agricultural Suppliers:** Suppliers in the agricultural industry provide raw materials such as seeds, fertilizers, and pesticides to support crop cultivation.
13. **Pharmaceutical Ingredient Suppliers:** The pharmaceutical industry relies on suppliers of raw materials, including active pharmaceutical ingredients (APIs) and excipients, for drug manufacturing.
14. **Recycling Centers:** In addition to primary raw material suppliers, recycling centers play a role by providing secondary raw materials obtained through the recycling of products and

materials.

Suppliers of raw materials are essential partners in the supply chain of many industries, and their reliability and quality of materials can significantly impact the production processes and final product quality of businesses in these sectors. Effective management of relationships with raw material suppliers is critical for ensuring a smooth production process and maintaining product quality.

Product manufacturing industry

The product manufacturing industry encompasses a broad range of businesses involved in the transformation of raw materials, components, or parts into finished products that are then sold to consumers or other businesses. This industry is a fundamental driver of economic growth and includes various sectors that produce an extensive array of products. Here are some key aspects and sectors within the product manufacturing industry:

1. **Diverse Range of Products:** The product manufacturing industry spans a wide range of products, including automobiles, electronics, textiles, food and beverages, machinery, chemicals, consumer goods, and more. These products can be both durable (e.g., appliances, vehicles) and non-durable (e.g., food, clothing).
2. **Production Processes:** Manufacturing processes vary depending on the product type but can include assembly, machining, molding, casting, chemical synthesis, and more. Automation and advanced technologies play a significant role in modern manufacturing.
3. **Quality Control:** Ensuring product quality is a top priority. Manufacturers employ quality control and quality assurance processes to meet industry standards and customer

expectations.

4. **Supply Chain Management:** Managing the supply chain is crucial for procuring raw materials, components, and parts, as well as distributing finished products efficiently. Effective logistics and inventory management are essential.
5. **Environmental Considerations:** Many manufacturers are increasingly focused on sustainable and eco-friendly practices, such as reducing waste, minimizing energy consumption, and using recycled materials.
6. **Regulatory Compliance:** Manufacturers must adhere to various regulations and standards related to product safety, environmental impact, labeling, and more. Compliance is essential to avoid legal and reputational risks.
7. **Global Supply Chains:** The globalization of supply chains has become common, with manufacturers sourcing materials and components from around the world. This globalization offers cost advantages but also introduces complexities in managing international logistics and trade.
8. **Technology Integration:** Manufacturers are adopting advanced technologies like robotics, artificial intelligence, IoT (Internet of Things), and 3D printing to enhance efficiency, reduce costs, and improve product quality.
9. **Customization:** Some manufacturers offer customization options to meet specific customer demands. This trend is particularly prominent in industries like automotive and consumer electronics.
10. **Lean Manufacturing:** The adoption of lean principles, such as minimizing waste and optimizing processes, has become a common practice to improve efficiency and competitiveness.
11. **Just-In-Time (JIT) Manufacturing:** JIT manufacturing focuses on minimizing inventory and production lead times, enabling manufacturers to respond quickly to changes in

demand.

12. **Safety and Employee Training:** Workplace safety is a critical concern in manufacturing, and employee training programs are essential to ensure a safe working environment.
13. **Research and Development (R&D):** Many manufacturers invest in R&D to innovate and develop new products or improve existing ones.
14. **Competition:** Manufacturers face intense competition, both domestically and globally. Staying competitive often requires innovation, cost control, and the ability to adapt to changing market conditions.
15. **Emerging Trends:** The industry is influenced by emerging trends, such as Industry 4.0 (the fourth industrial revolution), which emphasizes the integration of digital technologies into manufacturing processes.

The product manufacturing industry is a cornerstone of the global economy, contributing to job creation, technological advancement, and the production of a vast array of goods that enhance our daily lives. It is characterized by diversity, innovation, and a constant drive for efficiency and quality.

Transporting organisations engaged

Organizations engaged in transportation play a crucial role in the movement of people, goods, and services from one location to another. These organizations operate various modes of transportation, such as road, rail, air, sea, and even space travel. Here are some types of organizations that are actively involved in transportation:

1. **Freight Carriers:** These organizations specialize in transporting cargo and goods. They can include trucking companies, railway freight companies, maritime shipping

lines, and air cargo carriers. Freight carriers are essential for the distribution of products and raw materials in supply chains.

2. **Passenger Transportation:** Organizations in this category focus on moving people. This includes airlines, bus companies, taxi services, public transit agencies, and ride-sharing platforms. They provide transportation options for daily commuting, travel, and tourism.
3. **Logistics and Supply Chain Management:** Logistics companies coordinate the movement of goods, often integrating various modes of transportation. They offer services such as warehousing, inventory management, and distribution to ensure the efficient flow of products.
4. **Shipping and Freight Forwarding Agents:** These intermediaries facilitate international trade by arranging transportation, customs clearance, and documentation for shipments. They act as intermediaries between shippers and carriers.
5. **Railway Companies:** Railway organizations operate trains for both freight and passenger transportation. They transport goods over long distances efficiently and are often a sustainable transportation option.
6. **Airlines:** Airlines provide domestic and international passenger and cargo transportation services by air. They connect distant locations and play a vital role in global travel and trade.
7. **Maritime Shipping Companies:** Maritime shipping lines operate cargo vessels, container ships, and tankers to transport goods across oceans and seas. They are essential for international trade, especially for bulky or heavy cargo.
8. **Courier and Parcel Delivery Services:** These organizations focus on small package and document delivery. Examples include companies like FedEx, UPS, DHL, and national

postal services.

9. **Public Transit Authorities:** Public transit organizations operate buses, subways, trams, and commuter trains in urban and suburban areas. They provide affordable and accessible transportation options for residents and commuters.
10. **Rental Car Companies:** Rental car agencies offer vehicles for short-term use to individuals and businesses, providing flexibility and convenience for travelers and local residents.
11. **Space Travel Companies:** With the advancement of space exploration, private companies like SpaceX and Blue Origin have entered the space transportation sector, working on spacecraft and rockets for commercial space travel and satellite deployment.
12. **Automotive Manufacturers:** Although primarily known for producing vehicles, some automotive manufacturers are expanding into mobility services, such as car-sharing and ride-hailing platforms.
13. **Bicycle and Scooter Sharing Companies:** In urban areas, companies offer shared bicycles and electric scooters as eco-friendly transportation options for short trips.
14. **Transportation Network Companies (TNCs):** TNCs like Uber and Lyft connect passengers with drivers using smartphone apps. They have disrupted traditional taxi services and offer convenient ridesharing options.
15. **Cargo Airlines:** These specialized airlines focus on transporting air freight, including perishable goods, pharmaceuticals, and high-value cargo.

These organizations collectively form the backbone of transportation infrastructure, enabling the movement of people, goods, and services within regions and across borders. They play a critical role in facilitating trade, commerce, tourism, and daily life.

Market place and customers

A marketplace is a dynamic environment where goods and services are exchanged between sellers and buyers. Customers are the individuals or entities that participate in these exchanges by purchasing products or services from sellers within the marketplace. Here's a closer look at the relationship between marketplaces and customers:

Marketplace:

1. **Definition:** A marketplace is a physical or virtual space where sellers offer their products or services to potential buyers. Marketplaces can take various forms, including traditional physical markets, e-commerce platforms, online marketplaces, and brick-and-mortar stores.
2. **Types of Marketplaces:** There are different types of marketplaces, such as:
    - **Physical Markets:** These are traditional, physical locations like farmers' markets, shopping malls, and retail stores where customers can physically visit to buy goods and services.
    - **Online Marketplaces:** These are digital platforms where sellers list their products or services, and customers can browse and make purchases online. Examples include Amazon, eBay, and Alibaba.
    - **B2B Marketplaces:** These cater to businesses buying and selling products or services to other businesses, often in bulk quantities. Examples include Alibaba.com for wholesale trade.
    - **Auctions:** Auction platforms like eBay allow customers to bid on products, and the highest bidder wins the item.
    - **Service Marketplaces:** Platforms like Upwork and

TaskRabbit connect customers with service providers, such as freelancers or local service professionals.

Customers:

1. **Definition:** Customers are individuals, businesses, or organizations that purchase goods or services from sellers within a marketplace. They are an integral part of the economic system and are essential for the functioning of marketplaces.
2. **Types of Customers:** Customers can be categorized in various ways:
    - **B2C (Business-to-Consumer):** These are individual consumers who buy products or services for personal use. They shop for items like clothing, electronics, groceries, and more.
    - **B2B (Business-to-Business):** These are businesses or organizations that purchase products or services to support their operations or resale. B2B customers often buy in larger quantities.
    - **C2C (Consumer-to-Consumer):** In C2C transactions, individual consumers sell products or services to other individual consumers. Online platforms like eBay and Craigslist facilitate C2C transactions.
    - **Government and Institutional Buyers:** Governments, educational institutions, and nonprofits are also customers when they acquire goods and services for their operations.
3. **Customer Behavior:** Customer behavior in a marketplace can vary widely. It includes activities such as product research,

comparison shopping, making purchase decisions, and providing feedback or reviews about products or sellers.

4. **Customer Satisfaction:** Customer satisfaction is a crucial factor for both sellers and marketplaces. Satisfied customers are more likely to make repeat purchases and refer others to the marketplace.
5. **Marketplace Dynamics:** The interaction between sellers and customers shapes the dynamics of a marketplace. Factors such as pricing, product quality, availability, customer service, and marketing strategies influence customer decisions.
6. **Marketplace Regulation:** Some marketplaces are subject to regulations that aim to protect customers. These regulations may include consumer protection laws, privacy regulations, and product safety standards.

In summary, marketplaces serve as platforms where customers can access a wide range of products and services offered by sellers. Customers, in turn, contribute to the success of marketplaces by making purchases, providing feedback, and driving demand for goods and services within the marketplace ecosystem. Understanding customer preferences and behavior is crucial for both sellers and marketplaces to thrive in a competitive marketplace environment.

Warehousing

Warehousing is a critical component of logistics and supply chain management that involves the storage, handling, and management of goods and products. Warehouses serve as storage facilities where items are kept before they are shipped to their final destinations. Here's an overview of warehousing and its key functions:

Key Functions of Warehousing:

1. **Storage:** The primary function of a warehouse is to provide

secure storage for a wide range of products and materials. Warehouses are equipped with various storage systems, including shelving, pallet racks, and automated storage and retrieval systems (AS/RS), to accommodate different types of goods.

2. **Inventory Management:** Warehouses play a crucial role in inventory management by tracking the quantity, location, and condition of products. This helps businesses maintain adequate stock levels, reduce stockouts, and prevent overstocking.
3. **Order Fulfillment:** Warehouses are involved in the picking, packing, and shipping of products to fulfill customer orders. Efficient order fulfillment processes ensure that products are shipped accurately and on time.
4. **Consolidation:** Warehouses allow for the consolidation of goods from multiple suppliers or production facilities. This consolidation reduces transportation costs and improves the efficiency of distribution.
5. **Cross-Docking:** Some warehouses use cross-docking techniques, where incoming goods are transferred directly to outbound shipping vehicles without being stored. This approach minimizes storage time and speeds up the distribution process.
6. **Value-Added Services:** Warehouses often offer value-added services such as labeling, repackaging, kitting, and quality inspections. These services add value to products and meet specific customer requirements.
7. **Safety and Security:** Warehouses are responsible for maintaining a safe and secure environment for stored goods. This includes implementing security measures, fire prevention systems, and climate control when necessary.
8. **Distribution:** Warehouses are strategically located within

supply chains to facilitate the distribution of products to customers, retailers, or other distribution centers. They help reduce transit times and transportation costs.

9. **Reverse Logistics:** Warehouses also handle the reverse logistics process, which involves receiving, inspecting, and processing returned goods. This is important for product returns, repairs, recycling, or disposal.
10. **Documentation and Record-Keeping:** Warehouses maintain records related to inventory levels, inbound and outbound shipments, and product condition. This information is crucial for accurate accounting and compliance purposes.
11. **Technology Integration:** Many modern warehouses use advanced technologies such as warehouse management systems (WMS), barcoding, RFID (Radio-Frequency Identification), and automation to streamline operations and improve accuracy.
12. **Sustainability:** Sustainable warehousing practices aim to reduce energy consumption, minimize waste, and lower the environmental impact of warehouse operations. This may include energy-efficient lighting, waste recycling, and eco-friendly packaging.

Warehousing is a critical link in the supply chain, ensuring that products are stored and handled efficiently to meet customer demand while minimizing costs and ensuring product quality. Effective warehousing strategies are essential for businesses to remain competitive in today's global marketplace.

Basis of Documentation explanation

Documentation in the context of logistics refers to the process of creating, managing, and maintaining written, digital, or physical records and paperwork related to the movement, storage, and handling of goods and materials within the supply chain.

The basis of documentation refers to the fundamental principles and reasons behind the creation and maintenance of records, documents, and written records within various contexts, such as business, government, education, and research. Documentation serves as a means of recording information, facilitating communication, ensuring accountability, and preserving knowledge. Here is an explanation of the basis of documentation:

1. **Record Keeping:** One of the primary purposes of documentation is to create a record of events, transactions, decisions, or information. Records serve as historical evidence and help establish a factual account of what occurred, when it happened, and who was involved. This is crucial for legal, compliance, and audit purposes.
2. **Communication:** Documentation serves as a medium for communication, allowing individuals, organizations, and institutions to convey information, instructions, policies, and procedures. Well-documented information ensures that messages are clear, consistent, and easily understood by the intended audience.
3. **Information Retrieval:** Documentation facilitates the retrieval of information when needed. By organizing and indexing documents, individuals and organizations can quickly locate specific information or data, saving time and effort.
4. **Decision-Making:** Documentation provides the data and information necessary for informed decision-making. Managers and leaders rely on documented reports, analyses, and recommendations to make strategic choices and solve problems effectively.
5. **Accountability:** Documentation establishes a trail of

responsibility and accountability. When actions, decisions, or transactions are documented, it becomes possible to attribute them to specific individuals or entities, which is essential for accountability and transparency.

6. **Legal and Regulatory Compliance:** Many industries and organizations are subject to legal and regulatory requirements that mandate the creation and retention of certain documents. Compliance with these regulations is often a legal obligation.
7. **Training and Knowledge Transfer:** Documentation plays a crucial role in training and knowledge transfer within organizations. Manuals, guidelines, procedures, and training materials help new employees learn their roles and responsibilities and enable knowledge sharing among team members.
8. **Historical Preservation:** Documentation preserves historical knowledge and cultural heritage. In academia, libraries, and archives, documents, manuscripts, and records are stored to ensure that future generations can access and learn from the past.
9. **Problem Solving and Analysis:** When faced with challenges, problems, or disputes, documentation can serve as a valuable tool for analysis and resolution. It helps identify the root causes of issues and supports evidence-based problem-solving.
10. **Risk Management:** Documenting risks, incidents, and safety procedures is crucial for managing and mitigating potential risks. Organizations use documentation to develop risk assessment strategies and contingency plans.
11. **Quality Assurance:** In manufacturing and service industries, documentation is used to maintain quality standards. Standard operating procedures (SOPs) and quality control documentation ensure consistent and high-quality outputs.
12. **Project Management:** Documentation is a cornerstone of

project management. Project plans, schedules, status reports, and documentation of project milestones help keep projects on track and within scope.

13. **Collaboration:** Documentation facilitates collaboration among individuals and teams. Shared documents and collaborative tools enable multiple stakeholders to work together, share feedback, and contribute to projects or tasks.

Overall, the basis of documentation is rooted in the need for accuracy, transparency, organization, and communication in various aspects of human activities. Effective documentation practices are essential for achieving goals, managing information, and ensuring accountability across diverse fields and industries.

Importance of documentation

Documentation is of paramount importance in various aspects of human activities, including business, government, education, healthcare, research, and more. Its significance lies in the many benefits it provides to individuals, organizations, and society as a whole. Here are some key reasons why documentation is essential:

- **Record Keeping**
- **Communication**
- **Accountability**
- **Legal and Regulatory Compliance**
- **Knowledge Transfer**
- **Decision-Making**
- **Information**
- **Historical Preservation**
- **Problem Solving and Analysis**
- **Risk Management**
- **Quality Assurance.**

- **Project Management**
- **Collaboration**
- **Transparency**
- **Knowledge Preservation**

In summary, documentation is a fundamental tool that serves diverse purposes across various sectors and industries. Its importance lies in its ability to capture, convey, and preserve information, ultimately contributing to effective communication, informed decision-making, accountability, and the advancement of knowledge and society as a whole.

Usage of documents and document assistant

Documents play a crucial role in various aspects of personal, professional, and academic life. They serve as a means to convey information, record events, communicate ideas, and facilitate decision-making. In this context, document assistants, such as AI-powered language models, can provide valuable support in the creation, management, and optimization of documents. Here's how documents are used and how document assistants can be beneficial:

Usage of Documents:

1. **Communication:** Documents are used for written communication, including emails, letters, memos, and reports. They convey information, instructions, and ideas between individuals and organizations.
2. **Record Keeping:** Documents serve as records of important information, transactions, and events. Examples include invoices, receipts, contracts, and meeting minutes.
3. **Knowledge Sharing:** In education and research, documents like textbooks, research papers, and study materials are used to

share knowledge and information among students, scholars, and educators.

4. **Legal Documentation:** Legal documents such as contracts, agreements, and legal briefs are used to formalize legal relationships and ensure compliance with laws and regulations.
5. **Project Management:** Documents such as project plans, schedules, and status reports are essential for planning, monitoring, and tracking the progress of projects.
6. **Marketing and Promotion:** Businesses use marketing documents like brochures, flyers, and advertisements to promote products and services to customers.
7. **Documentation of Procedures:** Organizations create manuals and standard operating procedures (SOPs) to document processes, guidelines, and best practices for employees.
8. **Creative Writing:** Authors, poets, and screenwriters use documents to write novels, poems, screenplays, and other creative works.
9. **Data Analysis:** In data-driven fields, documents are used to present findings, research analyses, and statistical reports.

Benefits of Document Assistants:

Document assistants, such as AI-powered language models, offer several benefits in the creation and management of documents:

1. **Content Generation:** Document assistants can generate text content, including reports, articles, and summaries, quickly and efficiently based on user input and specific requirements.
2. **Editing and Proofreading:** They can assist in proofreading, grammar checking, and editing documents to ensure they are error-free and well-structured.
3. **Content Suggestions:** Document assistants can provide

suggestions for improving the clarity, coherence, and readability of written content.

4. **Automated Summaries:** They can generate concise summaries of lengthy documents, making it easier for readers to grasp key information.
5. **Translation:** Document assistants can assist in translating documents from one language to another, facilitating international communication and localization efforts.
6. **Data Analysis:** In data-driven fields, document assistants can assist in data analysis, generating charts, graphs, and explanations of findings.
7. **Content Organization:** They can help with organizing and structuring documents, including creating outlines, headings, and subheadings.
8. **Document Search:** Document assistants can search for specific information within documents, making it easier to locate and reference relevant content.
9. **Time Efficiency:** Document assistants can significantly reduce the time required for content creation, editing, and formatting.
10. **Accessibility:** They can convert text into different formats, such as audio or Braille, to enhance accessibility for individuals with disabilities.

In summary, documents are essential for various forms of communication and knowledge sharing, and document assistants powered by AI technology can enhance the efficiency and quality of document-related tasks. They offer valuable support in content generation, editing, organization, and other document-related activities, making them a valuable tool for individuals and organizations alike.

Preparation of various documents and

process involved

The preparation of various documents involves a systematic process to create, format, edit, and finalize documents for different purposes and contexts. The specific process can vary depending on the type of document and its intended use, but here is a general outline of the key steps involved in document preparation:

1. Define the Purpose and Audience:

- Determine the primary goal of the document.
- Identify the target audience or readers for the document.

2. Gather Information:

- Collect all necessary information, data, and content that will be included in the document.
- Research and verify facts, figures, and details to ensure accuracy.

3. Choose the Document Type:

- Select the appropriate type of document based on the purpose, such as a report, memo, letter, proposal, presentation, or manual.

4. Plan the Document Structure:

- Create an outline or structure for the document, including headings, subheadings, and sections.
- Decide on the logical flow of information within the document.

5. Draft the Content:

- Start writing the document content based on the outline.

- Write clear and concise sentences and paragraphs.
- Use appropriate formatting, such as bullet points, numbering, and headings, to enhance readability.

6. Review and Edit:

- Proofread the document for grammatical errors, spelling mistakes, and typos.
- Check for consistency in formatting and style.
- Ensure that the content aligns with the document's purpose and audience.

7. Revise and Refine:

- Make revisions to improve the clarity, coherence, and overall quality of the document.
- Seek feedback from colleagues or experts if necessary.

8. Add Visual Elements:

- Include relevant visuals, such as charts, graphs, images, or tables, to enhance understanding and engagement.
- Label and caption visual elements appropriately.

9. Format and Style:

- Apply consistent formatting and styling throughout the document, including font type, size, spacing, and margins.
- Use a consistent style guide if available.

10. Citation and References:

- If the document includes references to external sources, cite them accurately using a recognized citation style (e.g., APA, MLA, Chicago).

- Create a list of references or bibliography at the end of the document.

11. Final Review:

- Conduct a final review of the document to ensure that all changes have been incorporated and that it meets the desired quality and standards.

12. Approval and Signatures:

- If required, obtain approvals, signatures, or endorsements from relevant parties or stakeholders.

13. File Management:

- Save the document with an appropriate file name and in a secure location.
- Consider version control to track revisions and updates.

14. Distribution and Sharing:

- Determine how the document will be distributed or shared with the intended audience.
- Choose appropriate distribution methods, such as printing, emailing, uploading to a website, or sharing via a document management system.

15. Follow-Up and Feedback:

- After distribution, monitor the document's effectiveness and gather feedback from readers.
- Be prepared to make updates or revisions based on feedback and changing circumstances.

Document preparation is a structured process that ensures the creation of clear, accurate, and well-organized documents that effectively convey information or achieve their intended goals. It involves careful planning, drafting, reviewing, and formatting to produce documents that meet the needs of both the document creator and the audience.

Types of document and Circumstance in which used in logistics

Logistics involves a wide range of documents that are used in various circumstances to manage the flow of goods and information throughout the supply chain. These documents play a crucial role in ensuring the efficient movement of products and compliance with regulations. Here are some types of documents used in logistics and the circumstances in which they are used:

1. **Bill of Lading (BOL):**
    - **Circumstance:** BOLs are used in shipping to document the shipment of goods from the shipper (supplier) to the consignee (receiver).
    - **Purpose:** It serves as both a receipt of goods and a contract of carriage. BOLs include information about the cargo, its destination, and terms of shipment.
2. **Purchase Order (PO):**
    - **Circumstance:** POs are issued by a buyer to a supplier to request the purchase of goods or services.
    - **Purpose:** They specify the products or services needed, quantities, prices, payment terms, and delivery details, helping to formalize the procurement process.

3. **Invoice:**
    - **Circumstance:** Invoices are sent by the seller to the buyer to request payment for goods or services.
    - **Purpose:** They provide a detailed breakdown of costs, quantities, and payment terms, helping to facilitate the settlement of transactions.
4. **Packing List:**
    - **Circumstance:** Packing lists accompany shipments and provide a detailed inventory of the items included in a shipment.
    - **Purpose:** They help with the verification of goods upon receipt, aid in inventory management, and assist in customs declarations.
5. **Shipping Notice or Advice (ASN):**
    - **Circumstance:** ASNs are sent by the supplier to the buyer to provide advanced notice of a pending shipment.
    - **Purpose:** They include shipment details, such as contents, quantities, and expected delivery dates, allowing the recipient to prepare for the incoming goods.
6. **Customs Declaration Forms (e.g., Commercial Invoice, Certificate of Origin):**
    - **Circumstance:** These forms are used for international shipments to comply with customs regulations.
    - **Purpose:** They provide information required by customs authorities, such as the value, origin, and classification of goods, to facilitate customs clearance.
7. **Delivery Receipt (DR) or Proof of Delivery (POD):**

- **Circumstance:** DRs or PODs are signed by the recipient upon delivery of goods.
- **Purpose:** They serve as evidence of successful delivery and may include details such as the date, time, and condition of delivery.

8. **Warehouse Receipt:**
    - **Circumstance:** Warehouse receipts are issued by warehouses when goods are stored on behalf of a third party.
    - **Purpose:** They confirm the storage of goods, their quantity, and ownership, making them valuable for inventory management and collateral purposes.
9. **Transportation Management System (TMS) Reports:**
    - **Circumstance:** TMS-generated reports provide insights into transportation and logistics operations.
    - **Purpose:** They help logistics managers track shipments, optimize routes, monitor carrier performance, and make data-driven decisions.
10. **Bill of Materials (BOM):**
    - **Circumstance:** BOMs are used in manufacturing to list the components and materials needed to produce a product.
    - **Purpose:** They guide the procurement of materials and help plan production schedules.
11. **Certificate of Insurance:**
    - **Circumstance:** Issued by insurers, this document confirms that shipments are covered by insurance against specified risks.
    - **Purpose:** It provides proof of insurance coverage and aids in claims processing in case of loss or damage.

These are just a few examples of the many documents used in logistics to facilitate the movement of goods, ensure compliance with regulations, and support efficient supply chain operations. The specific documents used may vary depending on the industry, mode of transportation, and international trade considerations.

Chapter-2 Raw Material Documents

Documents for raw material supplier

Raw material suppliers in various industries typically require specific documents to facilitate the procurement and supply process. These documents help establish clear terms, ensure the quality of raw materials, and maintain transparency in the supplier relationship. Here are some key documents often used in dealings with raw material suppliers:

1. **Purchase Order (PO):**
    - A purchase order is issued by the buyer (in this case, the manufacturer or company purchasing raw materials) to formally request the supply of specific raw materials from the supplier.
    - It includes details such as the type and quantity of raw materials, delivery location, agreed-upon price, payment terms, and delivery schedule.
2. **Supplier Agreement or Contract:**
    - A supplier agreement or contract outlines the terms and conditions of the business relationship between the buyer and the raw material supplier.
    - It specifies responsibilities, quality standards, pricing, delivery terms, warranties, and dispute resolution procedures.
3. **Quality Control Documents:**
    - These documents, such as quality control specifications or quality assurance manuals, detail the required quality standards for the raw materials.
    - They may include specifications for composition, physical properties, testing methods, and acceptance criteria.

4. **Certificate of Analysis (COA):**
    - Suppliers often provide a COA for each batch of raw materials supplied. It certifies that the raw materials meet specified quality and safety standards.
    - The COA typically includes test results, batch numbers, and information on compliance with regulations.
5. **Material Safety Data Sheet (MSDS) or Safety Data Sheet (SDS):**
    - If the raw materials pose any safety or health hazards, the supplier should provide an MSDS or SDS.
    - These documents contain information about the safe handling, storage, and disposal of the raw materials and details on potential hazards.
6. **Delivery Note or Packing Slip:**
    - When raw materials are shipped, a delivery note or packing slip accompanies the shipment.
    - It includes a list of the items being delivered, their quantities, and any special handling instructions.
7. **Invoice:**
    - The supplier sends an invoice to request payment for the raw materials supplied.
    - The invoice provides details such as the itemized costs, payment terms, due date, and payment instructions.
8. **Certificate of Origin:**
    - For international transactions, a certificate of origin may be required to confirm the country of origin of the raw materials.
    - It may be needed for customs clearance and to comply with trade agreements.
9. **Customs Documentation (for International Transactions):**

- If raw materials are imported or exported, various customs-related documents, such as commercial invoices, packing lists, and certificates, may be necessary to meet customs requirements.

10. **Record of Receiving and Inspection:**
    - Upon receipt of raw materials, the buyer's personnel may document the arrival and conduct an inspection to ensure that the materials meet the specified requirements and are in good condition.

These documents are crucial for establishing a transparent and efficient relationship with raw material suppliers. They help ensure the quality and compliance of raw materials, clarify terms, and provide a record of transactions for both parties involved in the supply chain. The specific documents required may vary depending on the industry, regulations, and the nature of the raw materials being sourced.

Documents for product supplier

When dealing with product suppliers, whether for finished goods or components, several key documents are typically involved to facilitate the procurement process, ensure product quality, and establish clear terms of the supplier relationship. Here are some important documents used when working with product suppliers:

1. **Purchase Order (PO):**
    - A purchase order is issued by the buyer (e.g., retailer, manufacturer) to formally request the supply of specific products from the supplier.
    - It includes details such as the type and quantity of products, delivery location, agreed-upon price, payment terms, and delivery schedule.
2. **Supplier Agreement or Contract:**

- A supplier agreement or contract outlines the terms and conditions of the business relationship between the buyer and the product supplier.
- It specifies responsibilities, quality standards, pricing, delivery terms, warranties, and dispute resolution procedures.

3. **Product Specification Sheet:**
   - This document provides detailed specifications for the products being sourced, including technical specifications, dimensions, materials, and other relevant details.
   - It serves as a reference for ensuring that the supplier's products meet the buyer's requirements.
4. **Certificate of Conformity (COC):**
   - A COC is issued by the supplier to certify that the supplied products meet the specified quality and safety standards.
   - It typically includes information on product testing, compliance with regulations, and quality control measures.
5. **Product Samples:**
   - Product samples may be requested by the buyer for evaluation and quality assurance purposes before placing a larger order.
   - Samples allow the buyer to assess product quality, design, and functionality.
6. **Bill of Materials (BOM) or Product Component List:**
   - In the case of manufacturers, a BOM lists all the components and materials required to assemble the final product.
   - It helps ensure that the supplier provides the correct components as specified.

7. **Certificate of Origin:**
    - For international transactions, a certificate of origin may be required to confirm the country of origin of the products.
    - It may be needed for customs clearance and to comply with trade agreements.
8. **Customs Documentation (for International Transactions):**
    - If products are imported or exported, various customs-related documents, such as commercial invoices, packing lists, and certificates, may be necessary to meet customs requirements.
9. **Quality Control Records:**
    - Suppliers often maintain records of quality control tests and inspections conducted on their products.
    - These records can provide evidence of product quality and compliance.
10. **Delivery Note or Packing Slip:**
    - A delivery note or packing slip accompanies the shipment of products.
    - It includes a list of the items being delivered, their quantities, and any special handling instructions.
11. **Invoice:**
    - The supplier sends an invoice to request payment for the products supplied.
    - The invoice provides details such as the itemized costs, payment terms, due date, and payment instructions.
12. **Record of Receiving and Inspection:**
    - Upon receipt of products, the buyer's personnel may document the arrival and conduct an inspection to ensure that the products meet the specified requirements and are in good condition.

These documents are essential for establishing a transparent and efficient relationship with product suppliers. They help ensure product quality, clarify terms, and provide a record of transactions for both parties involved in the supply chain. The specific documents required may vary depending on the industry, regulations, and the nature of the products being sourced.

Documents for transport organisations

Transport organizations, including carriers, logistics providers, and freight forwarders, deal with a variety of documents to facilitate the movement of goods, ensure compliance with regulations, and manage the logistics process efficiently. Here are some essential documents commonly used in the context of transport organizations:

1. **Bill of Lading (BOL):**
    - A Bill of Lading is a critical document in the shipping industry. It serves as a receipt of goods, a contract of carriage, and a title to the goods.
    - BOLs are issued by carriers to shippers and provide details about the cargo, the route, and the terms of shipment.
2. **Freight Bill or Invoice:**
    - Freight bills or invoices are issued by carriers to request payment for shipping services rendered.
    - They include information on the shipment, charges, payment terms, and instructions for payment.
3. **Transportation Agreement or Contract:**
    - A transportation agreement outlines the terms and conditions of the transportation services provided by the carrier.
    - It specifies responsibilities, rates, service levels, liability, and dispute resolution procedures.

4. **Proof of Delivery (POD):**
    - A Proof of Delivery document is signed by the recipient upon the successful delivery of goods.
    - It serves as evidence of delivery and may include details such as the date, time, location, and recipient's signature.
5. **Waybill:**
    - A waybill is similar to a Bill of Lading but is typically used for shipments that do not require the title of goods to be transferred.
    - It contains essential information about the shipment and is used for tracking and documentation purposes.
6. **Customs Documentation (for International Transport):**
    - International shipments require various customs-related documents, such as commercial invoices, packing lists, certificates of origin, and customs declarations.
    - These documents are necessary to comply with customs regulations and facilitate international trade.
7. **Cargo Manifest:**
    - A cargo manifest lists all the goods carried on a vessel, aircraft, or other mode of transportation.
    - It provides details about the cargo, including quantity, weight, and description.
8. **Insurance Certificate (Cargo Insurance):**
    - An insurance certificate provides evidence of cargo insurance coverage for potential loss or damage during transit.
    - It may be required for international shipments and is crucial for risk management.

9. **Transportation Management System (TMS) Reports:**
    - TMS-generated reports provide insights into transportation and logistics operations.
    - They help transport organizations track shipments, optimize routes, monitor carrier performance, and make data-driven decisions.
10. **Load Tender and Confirmation:**
    - A load tender is issued by the shipper to request transportation services for a specific shipment.
    - The carrier responds with a confirmation, agreeing to transport the load.
11. **Hazmat Shipping Documents:**
    - If transporting hazardous materials, carriers must adhere to regulations and provide documents like a Hazardous Materials Shipping Paper.
12. **Certificate of Inspection (for Perishable Goods):**
    - For perishable cargo, a certificate of inspection may be required to confirm the quality and condition of the goods.
13. **Empty Container Return Receipt:**
    - When containers are returned to a carrier or leasing company, a receipt is issued to confirm the return.

These documents are vital for the efficient operation of transport organizations, compliance with regulations, and the management of shipments throughout the logistics process. The specific documents required may vary based on the mode of transportation, the nature of the cargo, and the international or domestic context of the transport operation.

Warehousing Import / export documents

Warehousing facilities, particularly those involved in import and export activities, deal with various documents to manage inventory, facilitate customs clearance, and ensure the efficient flow of goods through the supply chain. Here are some crucial import/export documents often used in warehousing:

Import Documents:

1. **Bill of Lading (BOL) or Airway Bill (AWB):**
   - A BOL or AWB is issued by the carrier to the consignee and serves as evidence of the shipment's arrival.
   - It includes details about the cargo, its origin, destination, and terms of shipment.
2. **Import License or Permit:**
   - An import license or permit may be required by the importing country's authorities to allow the entry of specific goods.
   - It ensures compliance with import regulations and may include product-specific requirements.
3. **Commercial Invoice:**
   - A commercial invoice is issued by the foreign seller and provides a detailed breakdown of the imported goods, including their value, quantity, and description.
   - It is a key document for customs purposes and payment.
4. **Packing List:**
   - A packing list accompanies the shipment and itemizes the contents, packaging details, and weights of each package or container.
   - It helps with customs clearance and inventory

management.

5. **Certificate of Origin:**
    - A certificate of origin confirms the country where the imported goods were produced or manufactured.
    - It may be required to determine eligibility for preferential trade agreements or tariffs.
6. **Customs Entry or Import Declaration:**
    - The customs entry or import declaration is submitted to customs authorities and provides information about the imported goods, their classification, and value.
    - It is essential for customs clearance and compliance.
7. **Importer Security Filing (ISF) or 10+2:**
    - For imports to the United States, an ISF filing is required to provide advance information about the shipment to U.S. Customs and Border Protection.
8. **Delivery Order (DO):**
    - A DO is issued by the carrier or freight forwarder to authorize the release of cargo from the port or terminal to the consignee or their agent.

Export Documents:

1. **Export License or Permit:**
    - An export license or permit may be required by the exporting country's authorities to authorize the export of specific goods.
    - It ensures compliance with export regulations and may include product-specific restrictions.
2. **Commercial Invoice:**
    - An export commercial invoice is issued by the seller and provides details about the exported goods, including their value, quantity, and description.

   - It serves as a basis for customs declaration and payment.
3. **Packing List:**
   - A packing list itemizes the contents, packaging details, and weights of each package or container being exported.
   - It helps with customs clearance and provides essential shipment details.
4. **Bill of Lading (BOL) or Airway Bill (AWB):**
   - A BOL or AWB is issued by the carrier and serves as a receipt for the goods being transported.
   - It includes information about the shipment's origin, destination, and terms of transportation.
5. **Certificate of Origin:**
   - A certificate of origin confirms the country where the exported goods were produced or manufactured.
   - It may be required to satisfy import regulations in the destination country.
6. **Export Declaration:**
   - The export declaration is submitted to customs authorities and provides information about the exported goods, their classification, and value.
   - It is essential for customs clearance and export control compliance.
7. **Shipper's Export Declaration (SED):**
   - In the United States, an SED is used to report exports and is submitted to the U.S. Census Bureau.
8. **Export Packing List:**
   - An export packing list provides more detailed packaging information and is often required for international shipments.
9. **Certificate of Inspection (if required):**

- Some products may require a certificate of inspection to confirm compliance with quality or safety standards.

These documents are integral to the import/export process and play a crucial role in customs clearance, regulatory compliance, and the efficient handling of goods within warehousing and distribution centers. The specific documents needed depend on factors such as the nature of the goods, destination, and relevant trade regulations.

Documents for inland traders and Overseas traders

Inland traders (those involved in domestic trade within a single country) and overseas traders (those engaged in international trade across borders) both require specific sets of documents to conduct their trade activities efficiently and in compliance with applicable regulations. Here are key documents commonly used by both types of traders:

Common Documents for Inland Traders and Overseas Traders:

1. **Invoice:**
    - An invoice is a fundamental document issued by a seller to a buyer. It provides a detailed breakdown of the goods or services sold, their quantity, unit price, total price, payment terms, and seller and buyer information.
    - In international trade, an invoice may include additional details for customs and tax purposes.
2. **Purchase Order (PO):**
    - A purchase order is issued by a buyer to a seller to formally request the purchase of goods or services. It specifies the products, quantities, prices, delivery

terms, and other terms and conditions.
- Both inland and overseas traders use purchase orders to initiate transactions.

3. **Delivery Note or Packing Slip:**
    - A delivery note or packing slip accompanies shipments and lists the items included in a delivery, their quantities, and any special instructions.
    - It is used for internal record-keeping and to help recipients verify the contents of a shipment.
4. **Payment Receipt:**
    - A payment receipt acknowledges that a payment has been made by the buyer to the seller. It includes payment details, such as the amount, date, payment method, and a reference to the corresponding invoice or transaction.
    - Receipts are essential for tracking payments and ensuring financial transparency.
5. **Certificate of Origin:**
    - A certificate of origin certifies the country in which the goods were produced or manufactured. It may be required for customs clearance and to qualify for preferential trade agreements.
    - This document is particularly important for overseas traders engaged in international trade.
6. **Bill of Lading (BOL) or Airway Bill (AWB):**
    - A BOL or AWB is a transportation document issued by carriers to confirm the receipt of goods, outline the terms of transportation, and serve as a title to the goods.
    - Overseas traders use these documents extensively for international shipments.
7. **Certificate of Compliance or Conformity (if required):**

- Certain products may require a certificate of compliance or conformity to confirm that they meet specific quality, safety, or regulatory standards.
- This document may be necessary for both domestic and international trade, depending on the product category.

Additional Documents for Overseas Traders:

1. **Customs Declaration Forms (e.g., Commercial Invoice, Packing List):**
    - Customs declaration forms, including the commercial invoice and packing list, are required for international shipments to provide information to customs authorities in the importing country.
2. **Export License or Permit:**
    - An export license or permit may be required for specific goods or controlled items when exporting to certain countries. It ensures compliance with export regulations.
3. **Import License (in the destination country):**
    - An import license may be required by the importing country's authorities for specific goods. Overseas traders must be aware of and comply with import licensing requirements in the destination country.
4. **Bill of Exchange or Letter of Credit (if used for payment):**
    - International trade often involves complex payment methods, such as letters of credit or bills of exchange, to facilitate secure transactions between overseas traders.
5. **Insurance Certificate (Marine Insurance):**
    - An insurance certificate provides evidence of insurance coverage for goods during transit,

protecting against potential loss or damage.
  - Marine insurance is crucial for overseas traders shipping goods across international waters.

6. **Export Declaration (in the exporting country):**
   - An export declaration is submitted to customs authorities in the exporting country to provide details about the exported goods and comply with export control regulations.
7. **Importer Security Filing (ISF) or Advance Commercial Information (ACI):**
   - For shipments to the United States, overseas traders must submit ISF or ACI data in advance to U.S. Customs and Border Protection.

These documents, whether used by inland or overseas traders, play a pivotal role in trade transactions, ensuring transparency, compliance with regulations, and effective communication between parties involved in the supply chain. Traders must be aware of the specific document requirements for their trade activities and the countries with which they are conducting business.

Documents required for Govt process,

Government processes often require a range of documents to ensure compliance, transparency, and the proper execution of various functions and procedures. The specific documents needed can vary widely depending on the nature of the government process and its purpose. Here are some common types of documents that may be required for government processes:

1. **Application Forms:**
   - Various government processes begin with the submission of application forms, which provide

essential information about individuals, businesses, or organizations applying for permits, licenses, benefits, or approvals.

2. **Identification and Personal Documents:**
   - Individuals often need to provide identification documents such as passports, driver's licenses, social security cards, or birth certificates to verify their identity and eligibility for government services.
3. **Business Licenses and Permits:**
   - Businesses may need to submit documents related to their legal structure, ownership, and compliance with zoning regulations to obtain licenses and permits for operation.
4. **Tax Returns and Financial Statements:**
   - Tax-related government processes often require individuals and businesses to provide tax returns, financial statements, and supporting documentation to report income, deductions, and financial status.
5. **Contracts and Agreements:**
   - Government contracts, procurement agreements, and grant applications typically involve the submission of legal documents outlining the terms, conditions, and obligations of all parties involved.
6. **Environmental Impact Assessments (EIAs):**
   - Certain projects, especially those with potential environmental impact, may require an EIA report detailing the project's effects and mitigation measures.
7. **Land Use and Zoning Documents:**
   - For property-related government processes, property owners may need to submit documents related to land use, zoning, property deeds, and land surveys.

8. **Building Plans and Blueprints:**
    - Construction permits often require the submission of architectural drawings, building plans, and engineering specifications to ensure compliance with building codes and safety standards.
9. **Certificates of Insurance:**
    - Businesses and contractors may need to provide certificates of insurance as proof of liability coverage for government contracts and projects.
10. **Health Records and Medical Certificates:**
    - Government healthcare processes may require individuals to provide health records, medical certificates, and vaccination records for various purposes, including immigration and public health.
11. **Education and Academic Records:**
    - Processes related to education, such as student visas or professional licenses, may require the submission of academic transcripts, diplomas, or certifications.
12. **Criminal Records and Background Checks:**
    - Certain government processes, such as immigration applications or job applications in sensitive positions, may require individuals to provide criminal records or undergo background checks.
13. **Certificates of Origin (for Trade and Import/Export):**
    - In international trade, certificates of origin may be required to verify the source country of goods and to comply with trade agreements and customs regulations.
14. **Immigration Documents:**
    - Immigration processes often involve a range of documents, including visa applications, passports, proof of employment, and sponsorship letters.

15. **Public Records and FOIA Requests:**
    - Individuals and organizations may request access to government records through Freedom of Information Act (FOIA) requests, which typically require a specific request document.
16. **Petitions and Public Comments:**
    - Public participation in government decision-making often involves submitting petitions, public comments, or responses to government proposals.
17. **Environmental and Regulatory Reports:**
    - Companies and organizations may need to provide environmental impact reports, safety assessments, and regulatory compliance documents for government regulatory processes.

These are just some examples of documents commonly required for government processes. The specific documents needed will depend on the nature of the government function or procedure and the relevant regulations and requirements. It's essential to check with the specific government agency or authority overseeing the process to ensure you provide the correct documentation.

Chamber of commerce

A Chamber of Commerce is a business organization that represents and promotes the interests of its member companies, typically within a specific geographic region or industry. Chambers of Commerce serve as advocates for businesses, provide networking opportunities, offer various services, and often play a vital role in supporting economic development and community growth. Here are some key functions and activities of a Chamber of Commerce:

1. **Advocacy and Lobbying:**

- Chambers of Commerce advocate for policies and legislation that support the interests of local businesses. They may lobby on issues such as taxation, regulation, trade, and infrastructure development.

2. **Networking and Business Connections:**
   - Chambers provide platforms for businesses to network with each other and build professional relationships. They often host events, seminars, and business expos to facilitate networking.
3. **Business Support and Resources:**
   - Chambers offer a range of resources and services to help businesses grow and succeed. This may include access to business development programs, mentoring, and educational workshops.
4. **Promotion of Local Businesses:**
   - Chambers actively promote their member businesses through various channels, such as directories, websites, and local marketing initiatives.
5. **Economic Development:**
   - Many Chambers of Commerce are involved in economic development efforts aimed at attracting new businesses, investments, and talent to their communities.
6. **Community Engagement:**
   - Chambers often engage with the local community through initiatives such as community service projects, sponsorships, and partnerships with nonprofit organizations.
7. **Information and Research:**
   - Chambers provide businesses with valuable market information, research, and data to help them make informed decisions.

8. **Government Relations:**
    - Chambers maintain relationships with local, state, and federal government entities to ensure that the voice of the business community is heard in policymaking.
9. **Events and Trade Shows:**
    - Chambers organize events, trade shows, and expos to showcase local businesses and stimulate economic activity.
10. **Education and Training:**
    - Some Chambers offer educational programs, workshops, and training sessions to enhance the skills and knowledge of business owners and employees.
11. **Membership Services:**
    - Chambers provide services and benefits to their member companies, such as access to health insurance plans, discounted services, and advocacy support.
12. **Visitor Services:**
    - Chambers often serve as a resource for tourists and visitors by providing information about local attractions, accommodations, and services.
13. **Certificates of Origin:**
    - Chambers may issue certificates of origin for goods being exported, which can be required for international trade.

Chambers of Commerce are typically funded through membership dues, sponsorships, and revenue generated from events and programs. They operate as nonprofit organizations dedicated to serving and strengthening the business community in their respective areas. Additionally, Chambers of Commerce can vary in size and focus, ranging from local or regional chambers to industry-specific chambers that serve a particular sector.

Certificate of origin

A Certificate of Origin is an official document that certifies the country of origin of goods being exported. It provides important information about the source of the products and is often required by customs authorities in the importing country to determine tariffs, trade preferences, and to ensure compliance with trade agreements. Here are key details about the Certificate of Origin:

1. **Purpose:**
    - The primary purpose of a Certificate of Origin is to establish the country where the goods were produced or manufactured. This information is crucial for customs authorities to apply the correct import duties and to verify compliance with trade regulations.
2. **Required for International Trade:**
    - Certificate of Origin requirements vary by country and trade agreements. Some countries or trading blocs, such as the European Union or the United States, may require a Certificate of Origin for certain imports.
3. **Contents:**
    - The document typically includes details such as the exporter's information, the consignee's information, a description of the goods (including their harmonized system code), the country of origin, and the signature and seal of the issuing authority.
4. **Issuing Authority:**
    - A Certificate of Origin is typically issued by a

recognized authority, such as a Chamber of Commerce, a government agency, or a trade association, depending on the country's regulations.

5. **Types of Certificates:**
    - There are various types of Certificates of Origin, including preferential certificates, non-preferential certificates, and certificates for specific purposes (e.g., re-export).
6. **Preferential Trade Agreements:**
    - In some cases, Certificates of Origin are used to qualify for preferential trade agreements or tariff reductions between countries. These certificates demonstrate that the goods meet the required criteria for preferential treatment.
7. **Legal Affirmation:**
    - The Certificate of Origin is a legal document. The issuer verifies the information and affirms that the goods originate from the declared country.
8. **Electronic Certificates:**
    - In many countries, electronic Certificates of Origin are becoming increasingly common. These digital certificates streamline the process and reduce paperwork.
9. **Customs Clearance:**
    - For the importing country, the Certificate of Origin plays a critical role in the customs clearance process. It helps customs authorities assess the correct duties and taxes and ensures that goods meet the necessary import requirements.
10. **Exporter's Responsibility:**
    - It is typically the responsibility of the exporter to obtain and provide the Certificate of Origin.

Exporters must ensure that the document accurately reflects the origin of the goods.

11. **Trade Documentation:**
    - The Certificate of Origin is an essential component of trade documentation, alongside other documents like commercial invoices, bills of lading, and packing lists.
12. **Fees and Processing Time:**
    - Issuing a Certificate of Origin may involve fees and processing time, depending on the issuing authority and the specific requirements.

A correctly completed Certificate of Origin is essential for facilitating international trade, ensuring compliance with customs regulations, and taking advantage of preferential trade agreements. It helps customs authorities determine the appropriate treatment for imported goods, which can impact their cost and eligibility for certain trade benefits.

Chapter-3 Documents for Transport

Proforma Invoice

A Proforma Invoice is a preliminary or provisional invoice provided by a seller to a potential buyer before the actual sale of goods or services. It serves as a formal quotation or estimate and is not a legally binding document like a commercial invoice. Here are key points to understand about a Proforma Invoice:

1. **Quotation or Offer:** A Proforma Invoice is essentially an offer made by the seller to the buyer. It outlines the details of a potential transaction, including the description of goods or services, quantities, prices, and terms of sale.
2. **Non-Binding:** Unlike a commercial invoice, which is used for an actual sale and creates a legal obligation for payment, a Proforma Invoice is not a legally binding agreement. It is a preliminary step in the negotiation and sales process.
3. **Use Cases:**
    - Proforma Invoices are commonly used in international trade to provide buyers with an estimate of costs, including product prices, shipping charges, and other expenses.
    - They are often requested by buyers to obtain import permits or financing.
    - Proforma Invoices are useful for securing letters of credit or other forms of payment assurance.
4. **Content:** A typical Proforma Invoice includes the following information:
    - Seller's and buyer's contact details.
    - Invoice date and a unique reference number.
    - Description of the goods or services, including quantity, unit price, and total price.

- Payment terms and methods.
- Shipping terms and estimated delivery date.
- Any additional terms and conditions.

5. **Customization:** Proforma Invoices can be tailored to suit the specific needs of the transaction. For example, they may include information about applicable taxes, customs duties, or other charges.
6. **Validation and Acceptance:** After receiving a Proforma Invoice, the buyer may review it and request modifications or clarifications. Once both parties agree on the terms, the Proforma Invoice may be converted into a commercial invoice for the actual sale.
7. **Legal Status:** Since a Proforma Invoice is not a legally binding document, it does not trigger tax liabilities or legal obligations. The actual sale and related obligations are established through a separate agreement.
8. **Record Keeping:** Both the seller and the buyer typically retain copies of the Proforma Invoice for record-keeping and reference purposes.

In summary, a Proforma Invoice serves as an essential tool in international trade and other business transactions by providing buyers with detailed cost estimates and terms before the actual sale. It helps both parties clarify expectations and negotiate the terms of the transaction. Once the terms are accepted, a commercial invoice is usually issued to formalize the sale.

Commercial Invoice

A Commercial Invoice is a legal document used in international trade and domestic transactions to record the sale of goods between a seller and a buyer. Unlike a Proforma Invoice, which is a preliminary quotation, a Commercial Invoice is a binding agreement that confirms the actual sale of goods. Here are key points to understand about a Commercial Invoice:

1. **Legal Document:** A Commercial Invoice is a legally binding document that serves as evidence of a commercial transaction. It outlines the terms of sale, the description of goods or services, and the agreed-upon price.
2. **Use Cases:**
    - In International Trade: Commercial Invoices are crucial for customs clearance, as they provide customs authorities with information about the goods being imported or exported.
    - In Domestic Trade: Commercial Invoices are also used for domestic transactions and serve as proof of sale for accounting and taxation purposes.
3. **Contents:** A typical Commercial Invoice includes the following details:
    - Seller's and buyer's contact details.
    - Invoice date and a unique reference number.
    - Description of the goods or services, including quantity, unit price, and total price.
    - Payment terms and methods.
    - Shipping terms and estimated delivery date.
    - Any applicable taxes, customs duties, or other charges.
    - Additional terms and conditions.
4. **Binding Agreement:** Once both the seller and the buyer agree to the terms outlined in the Commercial Invoice, it becomes a legally binding agreement that obligates the buyer to pay the specified amount for the goods or services.
5. **Customs Clearance:** In international trade, the Commercial Invoice is a vital document for customs authorities. It helps them assess the appropriate customs duties, taxes, and

regulatory compliance for imported or exported goods.

6. **Payment Reference:** The Commercial Invoice serves as a reference for payment. Buyers typically use it to make payment to the seller according to the agreed-upon terms.
7. **Record Keeping:** Both the seller and the buyer retain copies of the Commercial Invoice for their records. It is essential for financial and tax record-keeping purposes.
8. **Variations:** Depending on the specific requirements of the transaction and the regulations of the countries involved, Commercial Invoices may vary in format and content. Some industries and regions have specific requirements for the information to be included on the invoice.

In summary, a Commercial Invoice is a critical document in both international and domestic trade. It formalizes the sale of goods or services, outlines payment terms, and provides essential information for customs clearance and regulatory compliance. Unlike a Proforma Invoice, which is a preliminary estimate, a Commercial Invoice is legally binding and represents the final terms of a transaction.

Delivery challan

A Delivery Challan, also known as a Delivery Note or Delivery Slip, is a document used in the transportation and delivery of goods from a seller to a buyer. It serves as proof of delivery, confirming that the goods mentioned in the document have been dispatched or handed over to the recipient. Here are key points to understand about a Delivery Challan:

1. **Delivery Confirmation:** The primary purpose of a Delivery Challan is to confirm the delivery of goods. It provides evidence that the specified items have been transferred to the buyer or consignee.

2. **Non-Financial Document:** Unlike invoices or receipts, a Delivery Challan is not a financial document. It does not include payment details or prices. Instead, it focuses on the description and quantity of the goods being delivered.
3. **Contents:** A typical Delivery Challan includes the following information:
    - Date of delivery.
    - Name and address of the seller (supplier) and the buyer (consignee).
    - Description of the goods, including quantity, unit of measure, and any relevant product codes or references.
    - Any special handling or instructions related to the delivery.
    - The name and signature of the person making the delivery and the person receiving the goods.
4. **Proof of Receipt:** The recipient of the goods acknowledges receipt by signing the Delivery Challan. This signature serves as proof that the goods were delivered and received in the stated condition.
5. **Transportation Record:** In cases where goods are transported by a third-party carrier or logistics provider, the Delivery Challan may also include information about the mode of transportation, vehicle details, and driver information.
6. **Legal Status:** A Delivery Challan is a legally recognized document that can be used in disputes or claims related to delivery. It helps resolve disputes by providing a record of what was delivered and received.
7. **Invoice and Payment:** While a Delivery Challan does not include pricing information, it is often used in conjunction with an invoice. Once the goods are delivered, the seller

typically issues an invoice for the transaction, including the cost of the goods and any applicable taxes.

8. **Variations:** The format and content of a Delivery Challan may vary depending on local customs and business practices. Some industries or regions may have specific requirements for the information to be included on the document.
9. **Record Keeping:** Both the seller and the buyer maintain copies of the Delivery Challan for their records. It helps with inventory management, order fulfillment, and resolving any discrepancies.

In summary, a Delivery Challan is an essential document in the logistics and delivery process. It verifies the delivery of goods, provides a record of the transaction, and is a valuable tool for both sellers and buyers in ensuring accurate and transparent supply chain operations.

CST forms

CST forms, which stand for Central Sales Tax forms, are used in India to facilitate the movement of goods between different states in the country while accounting for the Central Sales Tax. The Central Sales Tax is a tax imposed by the central government on the sale of goods during inter-state trade. CST forms play a significant role in ensuring compliance with these tax regulations. Here are some key CST forms commonly used in India:

1. **CST Form C:**
    - Form C is issued by registered dealers to purchase goods at a lower CST rate (usually 2%) instead of the standard rate applicable to unregistered dealers.
    - It is used when goods are sold to another registered dealer located in a different state.
2. **CST Form E-I and E-II:**

- Form E-I is used for the export of goods from one state to another for the purpose of export to a foreign country.
- Form E-II is used for the export of goods from one state to another when the goods are intended to be used as raw materials for manufacturing and are eventually exported to a foreign country.

3. **CST Form F:**
   - Form F is used by a registered dealer to make tax-free purchases of goods for resale, manufacturing, or specified purposes in another state.
   - It is typically used for inter-state transactions between registered dealers.
4. **CST Form H:**
   - Form H is used for purchases made by diplomatic missions and United Nations organizations in India.
   - It exempts these organizations from paying CST on eligible transactions.
5. **CST Form I:**
   - Form I is used when the goods are transported from one state to another for job work, and the ownership of the goods remains with the sender.
   - It ensures that CST is not levied on the movement of goods for job work purposes.
6. **CST Form II:**
   - Form II is used when the goods are transported from one state to another for job work, and the ownership of the goods is transferred to the job worker.
   - It facilitates tax-free movement of goods to the job worker.
7. **CST Form G:**
   - Form G is used by the government or its agencies for

tax-free procurement of goods from another state.
   - It is applicable for inter-state purchases made by government entities.
8. **CST Form J:**
   - Form J is used when goods are sold to the Defense Department of the Government of India.
   - It exempts such transactions from CST.
9. **CST Form K:**
   - Form K is used for sales made to registered dealers who are engaged in the execution of works contracts.
   - It allows for concessional CST rates.

It's important to note that CST forms are subject to change based on evolving tax laws and regulations. Therefore, it is advisable for businesses involved in inter-state trade in India to stay updated with the latest CST form requirements and comply with the relevant tax laws to avoid penalties and ensure smooth transactions.

TIN services

TIN services, often referred to as Taxpayer Identification Number services, pertain to various functions and processes related to obtaining, managing, and using TINs in the context of taxation and financial matters. Here are some key aspects of TIN services:

1. **TIN Registration:**
   - TIN services often involve the registration process where individuals, businesses, or entities apply for a Taxpayer Identification Number. This number is essential for tax purposes and helps government authorities track taxpayers and their financial activities.
2. **Verification of TIN:**

    - TIN services may include online or offline tools to verify the validity of TINs. This verification process helps ensure that TINs provided by individuals or businesses are genuine and accurate.
3. **TIN Issuance:**
    - TIN services include the issuance of TINs by the relevant tax authorities. Once an application is approved, the tax authority assigns a unique TIN to the taxpayer.
4. **TIN Renewal and Updates:**
    - Taxpayers may need to update or renew their TINs periodically to ensure they remain valid and accurate. TIN services can facilitate this process.
5. **Lost or Forgotten TIN Retrieval:**
    - In cases where individuals or businesses have lost or forgotten their TIN, TIN services can provide assistance in retrieving or recovering the TIN.
6. **TIN Certificate or Card Issuance:**
    - Some tax authorities issue physical TIN certificates or cards to taxpayers as proof of their TIN. TIN services may include the issuance of such documents.
7. **TIN Application Assistance:**
    - TIN services often provide guidance and assistance to taxpayers in completing TIN application forms and ensuring all necessary information is provided.
8. **Tax Compliance Support:**
    - TIN services may offer resources and information to help taxpayers understand and comply with tax laws and regulations associated with their TIN.
9. **Online TIN Portals:**
    - Many tax authorities offer online portals or platforms where taxpayers can access TIN-related

services, including registration, updates, and verification.

10. **Reporting and Documentation:**
    - TIN services assist taxpayers in accurately reporting their financial information to tax authorities and maintaining the necessary documentation related to their TIN.
11. **TIN for Foreign Individuals or Entities:**
    - TIN services may also cater to foreign individuals or entities that have tax obligations in a particular country and need to obtain a TIN for compliance purposes.
12. **TIN for Business Transactions:**
    - In some cases, businesses may need to provide their TINs to other entities or government agencies for various financial and regulatory transactions. TIN services can help with these interactions.

TIN services are typically provided by government tax authorities or organizations authorized by tax authorities to assist taxpayers in matters related to Taxpayer Identification Numbers. These services are essential for maintaining accurate tax records, ensuring tax compliance, and facilitating various financial transactions and regulatory requirements.

Way bill

A Waybill (also spelled as "way bill") is a document used in the transportation of goods to detail the shipment's contents, origin, destination, and other essential information. It serves as a critical record and a contract of carriage between the shipper (sender) and the carrier (transporter). Here are key points to understand about a Waybill:

1. **Shipment Information:** A Waybill includes comprehensive information about the shipment, such as:
    - Names and addresses of the sender (shipper) and the recipient (consignee).
    - Description of the goods, including their nature, quantity, weight, dimensions, and packaging.
    - Origin and destination addresses, including any intermediate stops or transfer points.
    - Shipment reference numbers, tracking codes, or other identification.
2. **Contract of Carriage:** The Waybill acts as a contract between the shipper and the carrier, specifying the terms and conditions of the transportation service. It outlines the obligations and responsibilities of both parties.
3. **Non-Negotiable Document:** Unlike a bill of lading, a Waybill is typically a non-negotiable document. It does not represent ownership of the goods, and it cannot be used for transferring title to the cargo. Instead, it serves as evidence of the transportation arrangement.
4. **Proof of Shipment:** The Waybill serves as proof that the goods were handed over to the carrier in good condition and are in the process of being transported to the destination.
5. **Information for Customs:** Waybills often include essential information required by customs authorities for clearance purposes, such as the description of goods, their value, and the applicable tariffs or taxes.
6. **Tracking and Monitoring:** Many Waybills have tracking numbers or barcodes that allow for real-time monitoring of the shipment's status and location during transit. This information is valuable for both shippers and recipients.
7. **Electronic Waybills:** In modern logistics, electronic Waybills (e-Waybills) have become increasingly common. These digital

documents are generated and transmitted electronically, streamlining the documentation process and reducing paper usage.

8. **Multiple Copies:** Typically, multiple copies of the Waybill are produced. One copy remains with the carrier, one with the shipper, and others may be provided to customs authorities or other relevant parties.
9. **Waybill Number:** Each Waybill is assigned a unique identification number or code, allowing for easy reference and tracking throughout the transportation process.
10. **Delivery Confirmation:** The recipient (consignee) of the goods typically acknowledges receipt by signing the Waybill. This signature serves as confirmation that the goods were delivered in the stated condition and quantity.
11. **Legal Value:** Waybills have legal significance in the event of disputes or claims related to the shipment. They provide a record of the agreed-upon terms and conditions of transportation.

In summary, a Waybill is a crucial document in the logistics and transportation industry. It not only serves as a contract between the shipper and the carrier but also provides essential information for customs clearance, tracking, and proof of shipment. Whether in paper or electronic form, Waybills play a pivotal role in ensuring the smooth and organized movement of goods from one location to another.

Bill of lading

A Bill of Lading (BOL or BL) is a legal document issued by a carrier or their agent to acknowledge the receipt of cargo for shipment. It serves multiple purposes in the transportation and logistics industry, particularly in the movement of goods by sea, but it is also used in other modes of transport such as air, road, and rail. Here are key points to understand about a Bill of Lading:

1. **Receipt of Goods:** A Bill of Lading functions as a receipt, confirming that the carrier has received the specified cargo in good condition and is responsible for its transportation to the designated destination.
2. **Contract of Carriage:** It acts as a contract between the shipper (sender) and the carrier (transporter), outlining the terms and conditions of the transportation service. It defines the obligations and responsibilities of both parties.
3. **Title of Goods:** Depending on the type of Bill of Lading, it may serve as evidence of title to the goods. In the case of negotiable Bills of Lading, they can be used to transfer ownership of the cargo to a new party through endorsement.
4. **Types of Bills of Lading:**
    - **Straight (Non-Negotiable) Bill of Lading:** This type does not confer ownership of the goods and is not negotiable. It is typically used for shipments where the cargo is not intended to change hands during transit.
    - **Order (Negotiable) Bill of Lading:** This type can be negotiated or transferred to another party through endorsement and is often used in international trade. It enables the buyer to take possession of the goods upon presentation of the Bill of Lading.
    - **Bearer Bill of Lading:** This type allows the holder of the physical document to claim the cargo, similar to a bearer instrument.
5. **Contents of a Bill of Lading:** A typical Bill of Lading includes the following information:

  - Names and addresses of the shipper (consignor) and the recipient (consignee).
  - Description of the goods, including their quantity, weight, dimensions, and packaging.
  - Port of loading and port of discharge.
  - Vessel or transportation vehicle details.
  - Shipping terms, such as FOB (Free on Board) or CIF (Cost, Insurance, Freight).
  - Any special instructions or handling requirements.
  - Issuing date and Bill of Lading number.

6. **Functions in Cargo Handling:** A Bill of Lading is essential for cargo handling, including loading, unloading, and storage. It guides port authorities and stevedores in the proper treatment and delivery of the goods.
7. **Delivery of Goods:** The recipient of the goods typically needs to present the original Bill of Lading to claim and take possession of the cargo. This ensures that the cargo is released to the correct party.
8. **Legal Document:** In the event of disputes, damages, or insurance claims, the Bill of Lading serves as a critical piece of evidence, helping to establish the condition of the cargo at the time of shipment and the terms of the transportation contract.
9. **Electronic Bills of Lading:** In recent years, electronic Bills of Lading (e-BOLs) have gained popularity as a digital alternative to paper documents. E-BOLs offer efficiency, security, and environmental benefits.

In summary, a Bill of Lading is a fundamental document in the shipping and logistics industry, playing a central role in the transportation and delivery of goods. It serves as a receipt, contract, title document, and critical piece of evidence in international and domestic trade transactions.

Sea way bill

A Sea Waybill is a transport document used in international maritime shipping to acknowledge the receipt of goods and outline the terms of transportation. Unlike a traditional Bill of Lading, a Sea Waybill is a non-negotiable document, meaning it does not confer title to the goods, and it does not require presentation for the release of cargo at the destination. Here are key points to understand about a Sea Waybill:

1. **Receipt of Goods:** A Sea Waybill serves as a receipt issued by the carrier or its agent to acknowledge that they have received the specified cargo for shipment.
2. **Non-Negotiable Document:** Unlike a negotiable Bill of Lading, a Sea Waybill is non-negotiable. This means that it is not a document of title, and it does not allow the transfer of ownership of the goods by endorsement or physical possession of the document.
3. **Title to Goods:** Ownership of the goods is typically determined by other means, such as a sales contract or a separate negotiable instrument, rather than the Sea Waybill itself.
4. **Contents of a Sea Waybill:** A typical Sea Waybill includes the following information:
    - Names and addresses of the shipper (consignor) and the recipient (consignee).
    - Description of the goods, including their quantity, weight, dimensions, and packaging.
    - Port of loading and port of discharge.
    - Vessel details.
    - Shipping terms, such as CIF (Cost, Insurance, Freight) or FOB (Free on Board).
    - Issuing date and Sea Waybill number.

5. **Use Cases:** Sea Waybills are commonly used for shipments where the cargo is not intended to change hands during transit. They are often used for scenarios where the consignee has a pre-existing arrangement with the carrier and does not require the presentation of a negotiable document for cargo release.
6. **Advantages of Sea Waybills:**
    - Streamlined Process: Sea Waybills simplify the cargo-handling process because they do not require physical presentation for cargo release.
    - Reduced Risk of Fraud: Since Sea Waybills are non-negotiable, they are less susceptible to fraudulent transfers or disputes over title.
7. **Electronic Sea Waybills:** Similar to other shipping documents, electronic Sea Waybills (e-Sea Waybills) have become more common in modern logistics. E-Sea Waybills offer efficiency and reduce paperwork.
8. **Cargo Release:** In most cases, cargo can be released to the consignee upon proof of identity and confirmation of the consignment details without requiring the physical presentation of the Sea Waybill.
9. **Legal Status:** Sea Waybills are legally recognized documents that provide evidence of the terms of transportation and the receipt of cargo. They can be used in legal proceedings or disputes related to the shipment.

In summary, a Sea Waybill is a transport document used in maritime shipping to confirm the receipt of goods and outline the terms of transportation. It is a non-negotiable document that simplifies cargo handling, but it does not transfer ownership of the goods. Sea Waybills are especially useful for shipments where the consignee has a pre-existing agreement with the carrier and does not require a negotiable document for cargo release.

Customs Ice gate

ICEGATE, which stands for "Indian Customs Electronic Commerce/Electronic Data Interchange (EC/EDI) Gateway," is an online portal developed by the Indian Customs for the electronic exchange of trade-related information and documents between traders, customs authorities, and other stakeholders. ICEGATE plays a crucial role in facilitating international trade and customs clearance in India. Here are key points to understand about ICEGATE:

1. **Electronic Data Exchange:** ICEGATE is designed to facilitate the electronic exchange of trade-related data and documents. It allows importers, exporters, customs brokers, and other trade entities to submit and retrieve information electronically.
2. **Customs Declarations:** One of the primary functions of ICEGATE is to enable the submission of various customs declarations and clearances electronically. This includes documents such as Importer Exporter Code (IEC) applications, shipping bills, bills of entry, and more.
3. **Import and Export Declarations:** Importers use ICEGATE to file declarations for the import of goods into India, while exporters use it to file declarations for exports. These declarations include details of the goods, their classification, valuation, and other customs-related information.
4. **Digital Signatures:** ICEGATE supports the use of digital signatures, ensuring the authenticity and security of electronically submitted documents. Authorized personnel can digitally sign documents to verify their accuracy.
5. **Duty Payment:** Through ICEGATE, users can make online payments for customs duties, taxes, and other fees associated with the clearance of goods. This streamlines the payment process and reduces manual paperwork.

6. **Status Tracking:** Traders and customs authorities can track the status of their submitted documents and clearances in real-time through ICEGATE. This provides transparency and visibility into the customs clearance process.
7. **EDI Integration:** ICEGATE supports Electronic Data Interchange (EDI), allowing for the seamless integration of trade data with customs systems. This reduces data entry errors and enhances efficiency.
8. **Role-Based Access:** Users are assigned specific roles and permissions within ICEGATE based on their responsibilities. This ensures that authorized personnel have access to the appropriate functions and data.
9. **Customs Notifications:** ICEGATE provides a platform for customs authorities to communicate with traders and other stakeholders by issuing notifications, circulars, and updates related to customs procedures and regulations.
10. **Trade Facilitation:** ICEGATE aims to simplify and expedite the customs clearance process, reducing the time and effort required for traders to comply with customs requirements.
11. **User-Friendly Interface:** The ICEGATE portal is designed to be user-friendly, making it accessible to a wide range of users, including small and medium-sized businesses engaged in international trade.
12. **Data Security:** The portal is designed with robust security measures to protect sensitive trade data and ensure the confidentiality and integrity of electronic submissions.

In summary, ICEGATE is a vital platform for electronic customs clearance and trade facilitation in India. It enhances the efficiency of customs processes, reduces paperwork, and provides a secure and transparent environment for the exchange of trade-related information between stakeholders and customs authorities.

Rail goods way bill

A Rail Goods Waybill, often referred to as a Rail Consignment Note or Railway Bill of Lading, is a document used in the transportation of goods by rail. It serves as both a receipt and a contract of carriage between the shipper (sender) and the railway company responsible for transporting the goods. Here are key points to understand about a Rail Goods Waybill:

1. **Receipt of Goods:** A Rail Goods Waybill acknowledges that the railway company has received the specified goods from the shipper for transportation. It serves as proof that the goods were handed over in good condition.
2. **Contract of Carriage:** The Waybill functions as a contract between the shipper and the railway company, outlining the terms and conditions of the transportation service. It defines the obligations and responsibilities of both parties.
3. **Contents of a Rail Goods Waybill:** A typical Rail Goods Waybill includes the following information:
    - Names and addresses of the shipper (consignor) and the railway company.
    - Description of the goods, including quantity, weight, dimensions, and packaging.
    - Origin and destination points, including any intermediate stops or transfer points.
    - Railway bill number and date of issue.
    - Shipping terms, such as FOB (Free on Board) or CIF (Cost, Insurance, Freight).
    - Any special instructions, handling requirements, or hazardous materials information.
4. **Cargo Handling:** The Waybill guides railway personnel in the proper handling, loading, unloading, and storage of the goods during transit.

5. **Legal Document:** In the event of disputes, damages, or insurance claims, the Rail Goods Waybill serves as a critical piece of evidence, helping to establish the condition of the cargo at the time of shipment and the terms of the transportation contract.
6. **Cargo Release:** The recipient (consignee) of the goods typically needs to present the Rail Goods Waybill to claim and take possession of the cargo upon arrival at the destination. This ensures that the cargo is released to the correct party.
7. **Non-Negotiable Document:** Rail Goods Waybills are generally non-negotiable, meaning they are not transferable by endorsement or physical possession. Ownership of the goods is typically determined by other means, such as a sales contract.
8. **Electronic Waybills:** In modern rail logistics, electronic Rail Goods Waybills (e-Waybills) are becoming increasingly common. These digital documents offer efficiency and reduce paperwork.
9. **Role of Waybill in Cargo Tracking:** Many Rail Goods Waybills have tracking numbers or barcodes that allow for real-time monitoring of the shipment's status and location during transit. This information is valuable for both shippers and recipients.

In summary, a Rail Goods Waybill is a crucial document in rail transportation, serving as both a receipt and a contract of carriage. It outlines the terms and conditions of the transportation service, provides evidence of the shipment's condition, and is used for cargo release at the destination.

Entry tax form

An Entry Tax Form is a document used in some regions or countries to record and assess taxes on goods or commodities when they enter a specific jurisdiction or region. The purpose of an Entry Tax is to generate revenue for the local government and may be levied on goods imported from outside the region or those transported from one state to another within the same country. Here are key points to understand about Entry Tax Forms:

1. **Tax Assessment:** Entry Tax Forms are used to assess and calculate the tax liability on goods entering a particular jurisdiction. The tax amount is usually a percentage of the value of the goods.
2. **Types of Entry Taxes:** Entry taxes can vary from place to place and may be imposed by states, regions, or municipalities. They can include:
    - Entry Tax on goods imported from other countries into a specific region.
    - Entry Tax on goods transported from one state to another within the same country.
    - Entry Tax on certain categories of goods or commodities, such as luxury items or specific types of equipment.
3. **Registration and Documentation:** Importers or transporters are often required to register with the local tax authorities and submit Entry Tax Forms when bringing goods into the jurisdiction. These forms typically include details about the goods, their value, and the intended use.
4. **Rate and Calculation:** The rate of Entry Tax and the method of calculation can vary widely. Some regions may have a fixed rate, while others may base the tax on the value, weight, or volume of the goods.

5. **Exemptions and Concessions:** Certain goods or categories of businesses may be eligible for exemptions or concessions from Entry Tax. These exemptions can be based on the nature of the goods, their intended use, or specific government policies.
6. **Payment and Compliance:** Importers or transporters are responsible for paying the Entry Tax to the relevant tax authority within the prescribed time frame. Compliance with Entry Tax regulations is essential to avoid penalties or legal issues.
7. **Record Keeping:** Both the tax authorities and the businesses involved in importing or transporting goods maintain records related to Entry Tax, including Entry Tax Forms and payment receipts. These records are subject to audit and verification by tax authorities.
8. **Interstate Movement:** In some countries, Entry Tax can apply to goods transported from one state to another. Interstate Entry Tax Forms are used to document and assess taxes in such cases.
9. **Electronic Filing:** Many regions have transitioned to electronic filing and payment systems for Entry Tax, making the process more efficient and reducing paperwork.

It's important to note that the specific rules, regulations, and forms related to Entry Tax can vary significantly between regions and countries. Businesses involved in cross-border trade or interstate commerce should be aware of the applicable Entry Tax requirements in the jurisdictions where they operate to ensure compliance with tax laws and avoid any legal or financial consequences.

Octroi forms

Octroi forms are documents used in some regions, primarily in India, to assess and collect a local tax known as "octroi." Octroi is a tax levied by municipal or local authorities on goods entering a particular area or municipality, often a city or town. The revenue generated from octroi is typically used for local infrastructure development and public services. Here are key points to understand about Octroi forms:

1. **Tax Assessment:** Octroi forms are used to assess and calculate the octroi tax liability on goods entering a specific municipal or local jurisdiction. The tax is usually based on the type and quantity of goods.
2. **Types of Octroi Taxes:** Octroi taxes can vary between municipalities, and they may be applied differently based on local regulations. Common types of octroi taxes include:
    - Entry Octroi: Levied on goods entering the municipal area from outside.
    - Exit Octroi: Levied on goods leaving the municipal area.
    - Transport Octroi: Levied on goods transported within the municipal area.
3. **Registration and Documentation:** Importers, transporters, or individuals bringing goods into the jurisdiction are often required to register with the local octroi department and submit Octroi forms. These forms typically include details about the goods, their value, and other relevant information.
4. **Rate and Calculation:** The rate of octroi tax and the method of calculation can vary significantly from one municipality to another. Some may have a fixed rate, while others may base the tax on the value, weight, or volume of the goods.
5. **Exemptions and Concessions:** Certain goods or categories of businesses may be eligible for exemptions or concessions

from octroi taxes. These exemptions can be based on the nature of the goods, their intended use, or specific local policies.

6. **Payment and Compliance:** Those liable for octroi taxes are responsible for paying the tax to the local octroi department within the prescribed time frame. Compliance with octroi regulations is essential to avoid penalties or legal issues.
7. **Record Keeping:** Both the local octroi authorities and the businesses involved in importing or transporting goods maintain records related to octroi, including Octroi forms and payment receipts. These records may be subject to audit and verification by octroi authorities.
8. **Phasing Out of Octroi:** It's important to note that in India, octroi has been phased out in many states due to the introduction of the Goods and Services Tax (GST) in 2017. GST replaced various state and local taxes, including octroi, to create a unified tax system for the entire country.

Octroi forms and octroi tax systems are specific to certain regions and may no longer be applicable in areas where they have been replaced by GST or other tax reforms. Businesses operating in areas with octroi tax systems should be aware of the local regulations and requirements to ensure compliance with tax laws and avoid any legal or financial consequences.

Transit pass

A Transit Pass is a document or permit that authorizes the movement or transportation of goods or people through a specific area, jurisdiction, or country for a designated purpose, such as transportation, trade, or travel. Transit passes serve various purposes and can apply to different contexts. Here are some key points to understand about transit passes:

1. **Goods Transportation:** In the context of the movement of goods, a transit pass is often required for the legal and authorized transportation of goods from one location to another, especially when crossing international borders or traveling through specific regions. It helps ensure that goods are properly documented and accounted for during transit.
2. **International Transit:** For cross-border trade, transit passes may be used to facilitate the movement of goods through one country or customs jurisdiction to reach another. They are essential for customs clearance and compliance with import and export regulations.
3. **Transportation of Sensitive Goods:** Transit passes may be required for the transportation of sensitive or regulated goods, such as hazardous materials, firearms, or controlled substances. These passes help ensure that such goods are transported safely and in compliance with relevant laws.
4. **Customs Transit Procedures:** In international trade, transit passes are closely associated with customs transit procedures, such as the Common Transit Convention (CTC) in Europe. They allow goods to move through multiple countries without undergoing full customs clearance at each border, reducing delays and administrative burdens.
5. **Passenger Travel:** Transit passes can also apply to passengers traveling through specific areas or regions. For example, in some countries, travelers may require a transit pass or visa when transiting through an airport or crossing a land border on the way to their final destination.
6. **Temporary Movement:** Some transit passes are issued for temporary or short-term movement through a jurisdiction. They specify the duration and purpose of the transit, and they often come with restrictions on activities or stays within the transit area.

7. **Document Requirements:** Transit passes may come in various forms, including physical permits, visas, or electronic authorizations. The specific requirements and documentation may vary based on the nature of the transit and the regulations of the issuing authority.
8. **Customs Control:** Transit passes often involve close coordination with customs authorities to ensure that goods or travelers comply with applicable regulations and are properly monitored during transit.
9. **Transit Corridors:** Certain regions, such as transit corridors or economic zones, may have specific transit pass requirements to facilitate trade and transportation activities within those areas.
10. **Security and Compliance:** Transit passes help enhance security and compliance by ensuring that the movement of goods or people is tracked and monitored according to established rules and regulations.

It's important to note that the specific requirements and regulations regarding transit passes can vary widely from one jurisdiction or country to another. Businesses engaged in international trade or travelers planning transit through specific regions should familiarize themselves with the relevant transit pass requirements to ensure a smooth and legally compliant journey.

Packaging list

A Packaging List, also known as a packing list or shipping list, is a document typically included with a shipment of goods. It provides a detailed inventory of the items contained in the package or shipment. A packaging list serves several important purposes in logistics and shipping:

1. **Inventory Verification:** The primary purpose of a packaging list is to provide a comprehensive list of the items included in the shipment. It allows the recipient to verify that all expected items have been received and that they match the contents of the order.
2. **Shipping Details:** A packaging list often includes essential shipping information, such as the shipment's tracking or reference number, the date of shipment, the names and addresses of the sender (shipper) and the recipient (consignee), and the carrier's details.
3. **Item Description:** Each item in the shipment is typically described in detail on the packaging list. This includes information such as the item's name or description, quantity, unit of measurement (e.g., pieces, boxes, pounds), and, in some cases, the item's weight and value.
4. **Item Codes and SKUs:** Many packaging lists include item codes, SKUs (Stock Keeping Units), or other unique identifiers to ensure accuracy in identifying and tracking each item.
5. **Packaging Information:** The packaging list may indicate how the items are packaged, such as the number of boxes, pallets, or containers in the shipment. This information helps with handling and storage.
6. **Customs and Regulatory Compliance:** In international shipments, a packaging list may include details required for customs clearance, such as harmonized system (HS) codes, commodity descriptions, and the declared value of the goods.
7. **Reference to Other Documents:** The packaging list may reference other documents included in the shipment, such as an invoice or a Bill of Lading. This helps the recipient cross-reference and verify the accuracy of the shipment.
8. **Instructions and Special Notes:** Any special instructions,

handling guidelines, or important notes related to the items in the shipment may be included on the packaging list.

9. **Returns or Exchanges:** In some cases, a packaging list may include information on the return or exchange process, including instructions for returning items or reporting discrepancies.
10. **Record Keeping:** Both the sender and the recipient typically keep copies of the packaging list as part of their records. These records are useful for accounting, inventory management, and customer service purposes.
11. **Electronic Packaging Lists:** With the advent of electronic document management systems, packaging lists can also be generated and transmitted electronically, streamlining the documentation process.

A well-prepared packaging list is an important part of the shipping and receiving process. It helps ensure that shipments are accurately documented, that all items are accounted for, and that any discrepancies or issues can be quickly identified and resolved. In international trade, packaging lists are often required for customs clearance and regulatory compliance.

A Log Book and an R.C. (Registration Certificate) Book are two different documents related to vehicles, typically used for record-keeping and legal compliance. Here's an explanation of each:

Log Book:

- A Log Book, also known as a vehicle logbook or driver's log, is a document used to record detailed information about a vehicle's usage, maintenance, and service history.
- **Usage Recording:** The primary purpose of a logbook is to track the vehicle's usage, including trips, distances traveled, dates, and destinations. This information is often crucial for

businesses that use vehicles, as it helps monitor fuel consumption, route efficiency, and maintenance scheduling.

- **Maintenance Records:** Logbooks also include records of maintenance and repairs performed on the vehicle. This includes details such as service dates, odometer readings, parts replaced, and the names of mechanics or service providers.
- **Compliance:** Some industries and commercial vehicle operators are required by law to maintain logbooks to ensure compliance with regulations related to driver hours, rest breaks, and safety standards.
- **Tax and Accounting:** Logbooks can be used for tax purposes, as they provide a record of business-related vehicle expenses and mileage, which can be deducted from taxable income.
- **Security and Resale Value:** A well-maintained logbook can enhance a vehicle's resale value by demonstrating responsible ownership and regular maintenance.

R.C. (Registration Certificate) Book:

- An R.C. (Registration Certificate) Book, also known as a vehicle registration certificate or simply a vehicle's "RC," is an official document that serves as proof of vehicle ownership and registration with the appropriate government authorities.
- **Ownership and Identity:** The RC book includes essential information about the vehicle and its owner, such as the owner's name and address, vehicle identification number (VIN), engine number, chassis number, and details about the vehicle's make, model, and color.
- **Legal Requirement:** Vehicle registration and the issuance of an RC book are mandatory in most countries and regions. It confirms that the vehicle complies with safety and emissions

standards and is legally allowed to be driven on public roads.

- **Transfer of Ownership:** When a vehicle is sold or changes ownership, the RC book must be transferred to the new owner's name through a formal process with the local transport authority. Failing to do so can lead to legal complications.
- **Insurance and Accident Claims:** The RC book is often required for insurance purposes, and it is crucial when making accident claims or when a vehicle is involved in a legal dispute.
- **Validity and Renewal:** RC books typically have a validity period, after which they need to be renewed. Renewal ensures that the vehicle remains legally registered and compliant with government regulations.

In summary, a Log Book is primarily used to record vehicle usage, maintenance, and service history, while an R.C. (Registration Certificate) Book is an official document that serves as proof of vehicle ownership and registration with government authorities. Both documents play important roles in vehicle management, legal compliance, and record-keeping.

Tax Paid Certificate:

A Tax Paid Certificate is a document that serves as proof of payment of various taxes and fees related to a vehicle. These taxes may include road tax, vehicle registration tax, and other local or state taxes imposed by the government.

- **Purpose:** The primary purpose of a Tax Paid Certificate is to demonstrate that the vehicle owner or operator has fulfilled their tax obligations. It confirms that the necessary taxes and fees associated with the vehicle have been paid in compliance with local and national tax laws.

- **Registration Renewal:** In many jurisdictions, a Tax Paid Certificate is required for the renewal of a vehicle's registration. It is often a prerequisite to ensure that the vehicle remains legally registered and roadworthy.
- **Legal Compliance:** Holding a Tax Paid Certificate is essential for legal compliance, as it demonstrates that the vehicle owner is not in violation of tax regulations. Failure to pay taxes can lead to penalties, fines, or the suspension of vehicle registration.
- **Proof of Ownership:** The certificate may also include information about the vehicle's ownership and identification, helping to confirm the vehicle's legal status and ownership.

Transport Permit:

A Transport Permit, also known as a vehicle permit or transportation permit, is a legal authorization document that grants permission for the operation of a commercial or non-commercial vehicle for specific purposes, routes, or timeframes.

- **Purpose:** The primary purpose of a Transport Permit is to regulate and control the movement of vehicles, particularly in situations where there may be restrictions on certain types of vehicles, cargo, or routes. It ensures that vehicles are operated safely and in compliance with local regulations.
- **Types of Permits:** Transport Permits can vary widely based on their intended purpose. Common types include goods transport permits, passenger transport permits, oversize/overweight load permits, and special event permits.
- **Route and Timeframe:** A Transport Permit typically specifies the authorized route(s), dates of operation, and any

conditions or restrictions that apply to the permitted transportation.

- **Compliance:** Obtaining a Transport Permit is essential to ensure that the vehicle's operation aligns with local laws and regulations. Operating without a required permit can result in fines, vehicle impoundment, or other penalties.
- **Safety:** Transport Permits may be used to ensure that certain safety requirements, such as the use of warning signs or safety equipment, are met during transportation.
- **Cargo and Passenger Control:** In the case of goods or passenger transport permits, they may specify the type of cargo or the number of passengers allowed and may be subject to inspection by authorities.

Both Tax Paid Certificates and Transport Permits play vital roles in ensuring legal compliance and the safe and regulated operation of vehicles. They help government authorities track tax payments and enforce transportation regulations, ultimately contributing to road safety and revenue collection. The specific requirements and processes for obtaining these documents can vary by jurisdiction and the nature of the transportation activity.

Protection authentication

Protection authentication, in the context of security and information technology, refers to the process of verifying the identity of users or entities attempting to access a system, network, or sensitive data. It is a fundamental component of cybersecurity and data protection, helping to ensure that only authorized individuals or entities gain access to resources. Here are key points to understand about protection authentication:

1. **Identity Verification:** Protection authentication is all about

confirming the identity of users or entities. It ensures that individuals or systems are who they claim to be before granting them access to specific resources or privileges.

2. **Authentication Factors:** Authentication typically involves the use of one or more of the following factors to establish identity:
    - **Knowledge Factors:** Something the user knows, such as a password, PIN, or security questions.
    - **Possession Factors:** Something the user has, such as a physical security token, a smartphone, or a smart card.
    - **Biometric Factors:** Something unique to the user's physical or behavioral characteristics, such as fingerprint, facial recognition, or voice recognition.
3. **Authentication Methods:** There are various methods of authentication, including single-factor authentication (using one factor), two-factor authentication (2FA), and multi-factor authentication (MFA), which combines two or more factors for enhanced security.
4. **Access Control:** Once authentication is successful, access control mechanisms determine what resources or privileges the user or entity is allowed to access. This may involve role-based access control (RBAC) or permissions based on the user's identity.
5. **Security Measures:** Strong protection authentication involves using secure and well-implemented authentication methods and protocols. This includes the use of encryption to protect authentication credentials during transmission and storage.
6. **User Account Security:** Users are often required to create and maintain secure accounts, including choosing strong, unique passwords and regularly updating them. Password

policies may also be enforced to enhance security.

7. **Session Management:** Systems often manage user sessions to ensure that authenticated users remain authorized throughout their interactions with the system and are automatically logged out after a period of inactivity.
8. **Risk Assessment:** Some systems may incorporate risk-based authentication, which evaluates the risk level of an authentication attempt based on various factors (e.g., location, device used) and adjusts the level of authentication required accordingly.
9. **Biometric Authentication:** Biometric methods, such as fingerprint or facial recognition, offer a high level of security because they are based on unique physical attributes of individuals. They are increasingly used in smartphones and other devices.
10. **Passwordless Authentication:** Emerging technologies are moving toward passwordless authentication methods, such as using biometrics, mobile device authentication, or hardware tokens to eliminate the need for traditional passwords.
11. **Compliance and Regulations:** Many industries and organizations are subject to regulations and compliance requirements that mandate specific authentication and access control practices to protect sensitive data.
12. **User Education:** Users play a critical role in protection authentication. Education and training programs help users understand the importance of strong authentication practices and how to safeguard their credentials.

In summary, protection authentication is a foundational element of cybersecurity that involves verifying the identity of users or entities before granting access to systems or data. It relies on various authentication factors and methods to ensure the security and integrity of access controls, ultimately protecting sensitive information from unauthorized access and cyber threats.

Nature of goods transported

The "nature of goods transported" refers to the type, category, or characteristics of the cargo or products being moved from one location to another. It is a fundamental aspect of logistics and transportation management, as the nature of the goods has a significant impact on how they are handled, packaged, transported, and regulated. Here are key points to understand about the nature of goods transported:

1. **Diversity of Goods:** The nature of goods transported can vary widely, encompassing a broad range of products and commodities. These goods can include raw materials, finished products, perishable items, hazardous materials, consumer goods, machinery, and more.
2. **Classification:** Goods are often classified into categories based on their characteristics. Common classifications include:
    - **Perishable Goods:** Items that can spoil or deteriorate, such as food, flowers, and pharmaceuticals.
    - **Hazardous Materials:** Substances that pose a risk to health, safety, or the environment, including chemicals, explosives, and radioactive materials.
    - **Bulk Goods:** Commodities transported in large quantities without individual packaging, like grains, coal, or petroleum.
    - **Valuable Cargo:** High-value items such as electronics, jewelry, and currency.
    - **Oversized or Heavy Cargo:** Large or heavy

machinery, equipment, or construction materials.
  - **Consumer Goods:** Products intended for individual or household use, such as clothing, appliances, and electronics.
3. **Transportation Mode:** The choice of transportation mode (e.g., road, rail, air, sea) often depends on the nature of the goods. For example, certain goods may require refrigerated trucks for temperature-sensitive items, while oversized cargo may necessitate specialized transport equipment.
4. **Regulations and Compliance:** Different types of goods may be subject to specific regulations and compliance requirements. For example, hazardous materials must adhere to strict safety regulations, and the transport of pharmaceuticals may require temperature-controlled conditions.
5. **Packaging and Handling:** The nature of goods influences how they are packaged and handled. Fragile items may require specialized packaging for protection, while hazardous materials may need specific labeling and containment measures.
6. **Supply Chain Considerations:** Understanding the nature of goods is critical for supply chain management. It affects inventory management, order fulfillment, and the choice of distribution channels.
7. **Security and Insurance:** High-value or sensitive goods may require enhanced security measures during transport, and insurance coverage may vary based on the nature of the cargo.
8. **Customs and Documentation:** Import and export documentation requirements often depend on the nature of goods. Different categories may require specific permits, certificates, or customs declarations.
9. **Environmental Impact:** The transport of certain goods can

have environmental implications. For instance, the transportation of hazardous materials may necessitate adherence to environmental protection measures.

10. **Economic Factors:** The nature of goods can impact transportation costs, as certain items may require specialized handling or equipment, affecting pricing and logistics planning.

In summary, the nature of goods transported plays a crucial role in logistics and transportation management. It influences decisions related to packaging, handling, transportation mode, regulatory compliance, and various other aspects of the supply chain. Understanding and categorizing goods based on their characteristics is essential for efficient and safe transportation operations.

Weight of Goods Information:

- The weight of goods information refers to data about the total weight of the cargo being transported. This information is essential for several reasons:
    - **Safety:** Knowing the weight of goods is crucial for ensuring the safe handling and stowage of cargo within containers, trucks, or ships. Overloaded containers or vehicles can pose safety risks and affect stability during transport.
    - **Compliance:** Many countries and regions have weight restrictions and regulations for cargo transport. Providing accurate weight information is necessary to comply with these regulations, which may be enforced through fines or penalties.
    - **Transport Planning:** Accurate weight data is vital for transport planning, including selecting appropriate vehicles or containers, determining load distribution, and calculating fuel consumption.
    - **Cost Estimation:** Shipping costs, especially in containerized cargo transport, are often based on weight. Accurate weight information is

essential for cost estimation and billing purposes.

- **Methods of Determining Weight:** The weight of goods can be determined using various methods, including:
    - **Weighbridges:** Cargo is weighed on weighbridges or truck scales before being loaded onto vehicles or into containers.
    - **Load Cells:** Load cells or onboard weighing systems may be installed on vehicles to measure the weight of cargo during loading.
    - **Container Tare Weight:** For containerized cargo, the weight of the goods is calculated by subtracting the container's tare weight (empty weight) from the gross weight (loaded weight).

Container Safety Certificate:

- A Container Safety Certificate, often referred to as a Safety Approval Plate or CSC (Container Safety Convention) plate, is a mandatory certification for shipping containers used in international trade. It serves several important purposes:
    - **Safety Assurance:** The CSC plate indicates that the container has been inspected and meets safety standards for transportation. It ensures that the container is structurally sound and suitable for stacking and handling.
    - **Compliance:** The CSC certification is required for international shipments to comply with international regulations, including the International Maritime Organization's (IMO) guidelines. Containers without valid CSC plates may not be accepted for international transport.
    - **Identification:** The CSC plate includes essential information, such as the container's unique identification number (commonly referred to as the "container number"), maximum gross weight, and date of the last safety inspection.
    - **Responsibility:** The CSC certification is typically the responsibility of the container owner or operator. Containers must undergo periodic

safety inspections and be recertified when necessary to maintain compliance.

- **Inspections:** Containers are inspected by certified inspectors to ensure they meet safety and structural integrity standards. Inspections cover aspects such as the container's frame, floor, doors, and overall condition.
- **Validity:** The validity period of a CSC certification can vary by country and region. Containers must be re-inspected and recertified as needed to maintain compliance.

Health Certificate:

- A Health Certificate, also known as a Sanitary Certificate or Veterinary Certificate, is an official document issued by competent authorities, such as government health departments or veterinary agencies, to certify the health and safety of certain products, particularly food and agricultural items. Key points to understand about Health Certificates include:
    - **Food Safety:** Health Certificates are often used for food products, including meat, dairy, seafood, and fresh produce, to confirm that they meet specific health and hygiene standards and are safe for human consumption.
    - **Animal Products:** They are also used for animal by-products, such as hides, wool, or feathers, to ensure they do not pose health risks or carry diseases.
    - **Plant Products:** In some cases, Health Certificates are required for plant products to certify that they are free from pests and diseases.
    - **Export Requirement:** Health Certificates are often a mandatory requirement for exporting certain products to foreign countries. Importing countries may request these certificates to protect their own agriculture and public health.
    - **Inspection and Verification:** The issuance of a Health Certificate typically involves inspections, testing, and verification processes

carried out by government authorities or accredited agencies. The certificate confirms that the products meet the importing country's health and safety standards.

Customs Clearing Certificate:

- A Customs Clearing Certificate, often referred to as a Customs Clearance Document or simply a Customs Certificate, is a document issued by customs authorities or a licensed customs broker to confirm that customs procedures for imported or exported goods have been completed and that the goods are cleared for entry or exit from a country. Key points about Customs Clearing Certificates include:
    - **Customs Procedures:** Importing or exporting goods across international borders involves a series of customs procedures, including the assessment of duties, taxes, and compliance with trade regulations.
    - **Documentation:** To obtain a Customs Clearing Certificate, the necessary customs documentation must be submitted and processed. This may include the commercial invoice, packing list, Bill of Lading or Airway Bill, and other required documents.
    - **Tariffs and Duties:** Customs authorities assess applicable tariffs, import duties, and taxes based on the nature of the goods and their declared value. Payment of these charges may be a prerequisite for customs clearance.
    - **Compliance Verification:** Customs authorities may also verify that the goods comply with trade regulations, safety standards, and import/export restrictions.
    - **Release of Goods:** Once customs procedures are successfully completed, and any required fees or duties are paid, the Customs Clearing Certificate is issued, and the goods are released for entry into the country or for export.
    - **Licensed Brokers:** Customs clearing certificates can be obtained by importers themselves or by licensed customs brokers who specialize in navigating customs procedures on behalf of clients.

Warehousing Dues Paid Certificate:

- A Warehousing Dues Paid Certificate is a document issued by a warehouse operator or facility to confirm that all outstanding dues, fees, or charges related to the storage or handling of goods in a warehouse have been paid by the owner of the stored goods. Key points to understand about this certificate include:
    - **Storage and Handling Fees:** In warehousing, fees are typically charged for the storage, handling, and other services provided by the warehouse. These fees can accumulate over time.
    - **Dues Clearance:** The certificate serves as proof that the owner of the goods has settled all financial obligations with the warehouse operator, ensuring that there are no outstanding dues or debts related to the stored items.
    - **Release of Goods:** The certificate may be required before the stored goods can be released or withdrawn from the warehouse. It confirms that the goods' owner is in good financial standing with the warehouse facility.
    - **Record of Payment:** The certificate provides a record of payment and may include details such as the date of payment, the amount paid, the invoice or reference numbers, and the names and contact information of the parties involved.

Crew Qualification Certificate:

- A Crew Qualification Certificate, often referred to as a Seafarer's Certificate or a Maritime Qualification Certificate, is a document issued to individuals who work on ships, boats, or vessels, verifying their qualifications, training, and competency to perform specific roles and responsibilities at sea. Key points to understand about this certificate include:
    - **Maritime Roles:** The certificate is typically associated with individuals working in various maritime roles, including seafarers, sailors, officers, engineers, and other crew members.
    - **Training and Certification:** Crew members are required to undergo

specific training and educational programs to acquire the necessary skills and knowledge for their roles. The Crew Qualification Certificate is evidence that they have met these training requirements.

- **Safety and Compliance:** Maritime authorities and international regulations, such as the International Maritime Organization (IMO) conventions, mandate crew members to hold valid Crew Qualification Certificates as a measure to ensure safety at sea and compliance with international standards.
- **Roles and Responsibilities:** The certificate may specify the holder's qualifications and competency for particular positions, such as navigating officer, engine room personnel, deckhand, or other roles aboard a vessel.
- **Renewal and Validity:** Crew Qualification Certificates often have expiration dates and require periodic renewal to ensure that crew members remain up-to-date with training and competency requirements.
- **Global Recognition:** These certificates are recognized internationally, allowing crew members to work on ships that navigate in international waters.

Insurance policy(E Insurance)

An insurance policy, often referred to as "E-insurance" when it is electronically issued and managed, is a legal contract between an individual or organization (the policyholder) and an insurance company. This contract provides financial protection and compensation in the event of specified risks or losses. Here are key points to understand about insurance policies, including the electronic or digital aspect:

1. **Coverage Agreement:** An insurance policy outlines the terms, conditions, and scope of coverage. It specifies the risks or perils covered (e.g., auto accidents, property damage, health

issues) and the extent to which the insurer will provide financial protection.

2. **Premium:** The policyholder pays a premium, typically on a regular basis (e.g., monthly, quarterly, annually), to the insurance company. The premium amount is based on various factors, including the type of coverage, the insured's risk profile, and the policy's term.
3. **Policy Term:** Insurance policies have a defined term during which the coverage is in effect. At the end of the term, the policyholder may have the option to renew or modify the policy.
4. **Electronic Insurance (E-Insurance):** E-insurance refers to the digitization of insurance processes, including the issuance, management, and communication of insurance policies. This can include policies delivered electronically via email or accessible through online portals and mobile apps.
5. **Benefits of E-Insurance:**
    - **Convenience:** E-insurance offers policyholders the convenience of managing their policies online, including viewing policy documents, making premium payments, and filing claims electronically.
    - **Accessibility:** Digital policies are easily accessible from anywhere with an internet connection, making it convenient for policyholders to review their coverage details.
    - **Paperless:** E-insurance reduces the need for physical paperwork and allows for environmentally friendly, paperless transactions.
    - **Efficiency:** Claims processing and communication with insurers can be expedited through digital channels, leading to quicker responses and

settlements.

6. **Policy Documents:** An insurance policy typically includes several key documents:
   - **Policy Declarations:** These summarize the essential details of the policy, including the insured parties, coverage limits, and premium amounts.
   - **Policy Terms and Conditions:** This section outlines the specific terms and conditions of coverage, including exclusions, limitations, and deductibles.
   - **Endorsements/Riders:** These are optional additions or modifications to the standard policy that tailor coverage to the policyholder's needs.
   - **Exclusions:** Details of what is not covered by the policy, such as specific risks or events.
7. **Claims Process:** When a covered event occurs, the policyholder can file a claim with the insurance company. The insurer evaluates the claim, and if it meets the policy's criteria, compensation is provided to the policyholder or a designated beneficiary.
8. **Policyholder's Responsibilities:** Policyholders are expected to pay premiums on time, provide accurate information to the insurer, and adhere to the terms and conditions of the policy. Failure to do so can impact coverage and claims.
9. **Regulations:** Insurance policies are subject to regulations and oversight by government authorities to ensure fairness and transparency in the insurance industry.

In summary, an insurance policy, whether issued electronically or in print, is a legal contract that provides financial protection against specified risks or losses. E-insurance, or electronic insurance, enhances convenience and accessibility by digitizing policy issuance and management processes, making it easier for policyholders to access and manage their coverage.

In bound consignment process, outbound consignment process

Inbound Consignment Process and Outbound Consignment Process are two fundamental procedures in the field of logistics and supply chain management. They describe the flow of goods or products into and out of an organization or business. Here's an explanation of each process:

1. Inbound Consignment Process:

- The Inbound Consignment Process, also known as the Procure-to-Pay (P2P) process or the procurement process, deals with the acquisition of goods, raw materials, or products from external suppliers or vendors. It encompasses the steps from identifying a need for materials to receiving and managing those materials within the organization. Key aspects of the inbound consignment process include:
    - **Demand Analysis:** Determining the need for specific materials or products within the organization, often based on factors like production requirements, inventory levels, and customer orders.
    - **Supplier Selection:** Identifying and choosing suitable suppliers or vendors based on factors such as quality, cost, reliability, and delivery capabilities.
    - **Purchase Order (PO) Creation:** Generating a purchase order that outlines the quantity, specifications, price, and terms of the purchase.
    - **Order Confirmation:** Receiving confirmation from the supplier that they can fulfill the order as specified in the purchase order.
    - **Goods Receipt:** Physically receiving the ordered goods or materials at the organization's facility, verifying their quantity and quality, and

updating inventory records.

  - **Invoice Processing:** Reviewing and processing the supplier's invoice for payment, ensuring it matches the purchase order and goods receipt.
  - **Payment:** Settling the supplier's invoice according to agreed-upon payment terms.

- The goal of the inbound consignment process is to ensure a smooth and efficient flow of materials into the organization, maintain appropriate inventory levels, and optimize costs.

2. Outbound Consignment Process:

- The Outbound Consignment Process, also known as the Order-to-Cash (O2C) process or the sales and distribution process, revolves around the sale and delivery of products to customers or clients. It encompasses the steps from receiving a customer order to delivering the ordered products and receiving payment. Key aspects of the outbound consignment process include:
  - **Order Management:** Receiving and processing customer orders, which includes verifying product availability, pricing, and credit limits.
  - **Order Fulfillment:** Preparing and packaging the ordered products for shipment, including picking, packing, and labeling.
  - **Shipment and Delivery:** Arranging the transportation of the goods to the customer's location, tracking the shipment, and ensuring timely delivery.
  - **Invoicing:** Generating and sending invoices to customers based on the products delivered, prices, and terms.
  - **Payment Processing:** Receiving payments from customers, applying them to outstanding invoices, and managing accounts receivable.
  - **Returns and Customer Service:** Handling customer returns, addressing inquiries, and resolving any issues related to the delivered products.

- The primary goal of the outbound consignment process is to fulfill customer orders accurately and efficiently, maintain customer satisfaction, and manage revenue collection.

Both the Inbound Consignment Process and the Outbound Consignment Process are critical components of supply chain management, and their effective execution is essential for organizations to meet customer demand, manage costs, and maintain efficient operations. The two processes are often interconnected, as efficient inbound logistics support smooth outbound logistics, ultimately contributing to the success of a business.

Goods and Services Tax (GST):

- GST is a value-added tax system that is applied to the supply of goods and services in many countries. It replaces multiple indirect taxes with a single unified tax, simplifying the taxation process. Key points about GST include:
    - **Unified Tax:** GST eliminates the cascading effect of taxes by allowing businesses to claim credit for the GST paid on inputs and services used in the production of goods or services.
    - **Multiple Rates:** GST often has different tax rates for various categories of goods and services. These rates can vary from zero (exempt) to standard rates.
    - **Input Tax Credit:** Businesses can offset the GST they've paid on purchases against the GST they collect on sales, reducing their tax liability.
    - **Compliance:** Businesses are required to file regular GST returns, which detail their sales, purchases, and tax liabilities.
    - **E-invoicing:** Many countries have implemented electronic invoicing (E-invoicing) systems to ensure the accuracy and transparency of GST-related transactions.

Documents:

- Various documents are essential in the context of GST and the movement of goods, including:
    - **Invoice:** An invoice is a document issued by a seller to a buyer, detailing the products or services sold, their quantities, prices, and applicable taxes. It serves as proof of the transaction.
    - **Purchase Order (PO):** A purchase order is issued by a buyer to a seller, formally requesting the purchase of goods or services. It often includes specifications, quantities, and terms of the purchase.
    - **Bill of Lading:** This document is commonly used in the shipping industry and serves as a receipt for goods, a contract of carriage, and evidence of title to the goods. It is crucial in international trade.
    - **Delivery Challan:** A delivery challan is a document used to record the movement of goods within a state or between states. It often accompanies the goods during transportation.
    - **Payment Receipt:** A payment receipt acknowledges the receipt of payment from a customer or buyer for goods or services rendered. It includes details such as the payment amount, date, and method.

E-waybill (Electronic Waybill):

- An E-waybill is a digital document or electronic record generated online for the movement of goods. It is used to facilitate the seamless movement of goods within and between states, ensure tax compliance, and minimize tax evasion. Key aspects of E-waybill include:
    - **Mandatory Requirement:** In many countries, E-waybill generation is mandatory for the transportation of goods above a certain value threshold, both within a state (intra-state) and between states (inter-state).
    - **Information:** The E-waybill typically includes details such as the consignor's and consignee's information, the description of goods, their value, the vehicle number, and the route of transportation.
    - **Validity:** E-waybills are valid for a specific period and distance, depending on the transportation mode and the distance covered.

- ◦ **Electronic Generation:** E-waybills are generated electronically through government portals or authorized service providers. They often include a unique E-waybill number.
- ◦ **Inspection:** Authorities can verify E-waybills during transit to ensure compliance with tax regulations.

Documents relating to accidents and claims

Documents relating to accidents and claims are essential for the process of reporting, documenting, and resolving accidents, incidents, and insurance claims. These documents help establish the facts surrounding an accident or incident, assess liability, and facilitate the claims process. Here are some key documents related to accidents and claims:

1. Accident Report:

- An accident report is a formal document used to record the details of an accident or incident. It typically includes information about the date, time, and location of the accident, a description of what happened, and the names and contact information of individuals involved or witnesses. The report may also contain photographs, diagrams, or sketches to illustrate the scene.

2. Police Report:

- In cases where law enforcement authorities are involved, a police report is generated. It provides an official account of the accident, including the statements of involved parties, witness statements, and the officer's assessment of the scene. A police report is often required for insurance claims and legal proceedings.

3. Witness Statements:

- Witness statements are written or recorded accounts from individuals who observed the accident or incident. These statements can help establish the sequence of events, clarify liability, and provide additional perspectives on what happened.

4. Insurance Claim Form:

- An insurance claim form is a formal request submitted to an insurance company to seek compensation for damages or losses resulting from an accident or incident. The form typically requires the claimant to provide details about the accident, the extent of damages, and supporting documentation.

5. Medical Records and Bills:

- In cases involving personal injuries, medical records and bills are crucial. These documents include medical assessments, treatment records, diagnostic reports, and invoices related to medical expenses. They serve as evidence of injuries and the cost of medical care.

6. Vehicle Repair Estimates:

- If the accident involves vehicles, repair estimates from auto repair shops are essential. These estimates outline the cost of repairing the damage to the vehicles involved. They are used to assess the extent of property damage and calculate insurance payouts.

7. Proof of Loss Statement:

- A proof of loss statement is a formal document submitted to the insurance company that outlines the details of the claim, including the nature of the loss, the extent of damages or injuries, and the amount being claimed. It serves as a formal request for compensation.

8. Accident Reconstruction Report:

- In complex accidents, an accident reconstruction report may be prepared by experts. This report uses physical evidence, mathematical calculations, and engineering principles to reconstruct the accident's sequence of events and determine liability.

9. Witness Affidavits:

- Witness affidavits are legally binding statements made under oath by witnesses. They provide a sworn account of what the witness observed during the accident or incident and may be used as evidence in legal proceedings.

10. Settlement Agreements:

- If a settlement is reached between parties involved in the accident or between the claimant and the insurance company, a settlement agreement is drafted. This document outlines the terms of the settlement, including the amount of compensation and any release of liability.

11. Correspondence and Communication:

- All written and electronic correspondence related to the accident and claims process should be retained. This includes emails, letters, and messages exchanged with insurance companies, legal representatives, and other relevant parties.

Properly documenting accidents and claims is essential for transparency, liability determination, and the successful resolution of insurance claims and legal matters. These documents help ensure that all parties involved have access to accurate information and that claims are processed fairly and efficiently.

Chapter-4 Documents for sea transport

Documents for sea transport, also known as shipping documents, are essential for facilitating the movement of goods by sea and ensuring compliance with international maritime regulations. These documents provide a record of the cargo, its ownership, and the terms of the transportation contract.

These sea transport documents are critical for the efficient and compliant movement of goods by sea. The specific documents required can vary based on factors such as the type of cargo, destination, and trade agreements between countries. Properly completing and presenting these documents is essential to ensure a smooth and legally compliant sea transport process.

Bill of lading, Types,

A Bill of Lading (B/L) is a crucial shipping document used in international trade and maritime transportation. It serves as a receipt, a contract of carriage, and a title document for goods being transported by sea. There are different types of Bills of Lading, each with specific characteristics and purposes. Here are the main types of Bills of Lading:

1. Straight Bill of Lading (SB/L):

- Also known as a non-negotiable or non-transferable Bill of Lading.
- It specifies that the goods are consigned to a particular party, often the consignee named in the document.
- Typically used when the goods are pre-paid, and the shipper does not want the goods to be negotiable or transferable to another party during transit.
- It does not provide the consignee with the ability to transfer ownership of the goods to others.

2. Order Bill of Lading (OB/L):

- Also known as a negotiable Bill of Lading.
- It allows for the transfer of ownership by endorsement and physical delivery of the document.
- The consignee named can endorse the B/L to another party, making it a negotiable instrument. This facilitates trade and can serve as collateral for financing.
- Commonly used in international trade for transactions involving letters of credit and open account arrangements.

3. Bearer Bill of Lading (BB/L):

- This type of Bill of Lading does not specify a named consignee.
- It allows the holder of the physical document (bearer) to claim the goods.
- BB/Ls are relatively rare today due to security concerns, as they can be lost or stolen, leading to potential disputes.

4. Through Bill of Lading (T/B/L):

- A Through Bill of Lading is used when goods are transported using multiple modes of transportation, such as sea, rail, and truck.
- It covers the entire journey from the point of origin to the final destination and may involve multiple carriers and intermediaries.
- T/B/Ls are essential for ensuring seamless transportation and coordination among carriers.

5. Clean Bill of Lading:

- A Clean Bill of Lading is issued when the cargo has been received by the carrier in apparent good condition and properly packaged.

- It does not contain notations or remarks indicating damage, loss, or discrepancies in the cargo.
- It serves as confirmation that the cargo was in acceptable condition when received.

6. Claused or Foul Bill of Lading:

- A Claused or Foul Bill of Lading contains notations or remarks indicating exceptions or discrepancies in the cargo, such as damage or shortages.
- It may specify the condition of the cargo at the time of receipt and can be used as evidence in the event of a claim.

The choice of Bill of Lading type depends on the specific requirements of the shipper, consignee, and the nature of the transaction. It is essential for parties involved in international trade and shipping to understand the implications of different B/L types, as they can have significant legal and financial consequences.

Crew passenger health certificate

A Crew and Passenger Health Certificate is a document that certifies the health and fitness of individuals, such as crew members and passengers, who are involved in maritime transportation, particularly on ships and vessels. This certificate is an important aspect of maritime safety and public health regulations. Here are key points about the Crew and Passenger Health Certificate:

1. **Purpose:**
    - The primary purpose of the Crew and Passenger Health Certificate is to ensure that individuals on board a ship or vessel are in good health and do not pose a risk to others due to infectious diseases or medical conditions.

2. **Issuing Authority:**
    - The certificate is typically issued by qualified medical professionals, often approved or recognized by maritime authorities or relevant health agencies. These professionals may include ship's doctors or designated medical practitioners.
3. **Medical Examination:**
    - To obtain the certificate, crew members and passengers are required to undergo a medical examination. This examination may include assessments of physical health, mental health, and vaccination status.
4. **Testing and Vaccination:**
    - Depending on the type of ship and its itinerary, individuals may be required to undergo specific medical tests or screenings, such as tuberculosis (TB) tests or vaccinations against certain diseases.
5. **Validity Period:**
    - The Crew and Passenger Health Certificate typically has a specified validity period, after which individuals must undergo another medical examination to renew the certificate. The duration of validity may vary depending on local regulations and the type of ship or voyage.
6. **Infectious Disease Control:**
    - The certificate plays a vital role in controlling the spread of infectious diseases, as it ensures that individuals with contagious illnesses are identified and appropriate measures are taken to prevent outbreaks on board.
7. **International Travel:**
    - For ships engaged in international travel, the Crew

and Passenger Health Certificate may be required to comply with international health regulations, such as those set forth by the International Health Regulations (IHR) of the World Health Organization (WHO).

8. **Customs and Port Authorities:**
    - Customs and port authorities often inspect the Crew and Passenger Health Certificates to verify the health status of individuals on board. Non-compliance with health requirements can lead to delays or refusal of entry into certain ports.
9. **Public Health Records:**
    - Health authorities may maintain records of individuals' health status as part of public health surveillance efforts. These records can help identify and respond to outbreaks or health emergencies.
10. **Quarantine and Isolation:**
    - In cases where an individual is found to have a contagious disease, the Crew and Passenger Health Certificate may trigger quarantine or isolation protocols to prevent the spread of the illness.

Overall, the Crew and Passenger Health Certificate is an essential document to safeguard the health and well-being of individuals on maritime voyages and to prevent the transmission of diseases within the confined environment of a ship or vessel. It is an integral part of maritime safety and health regulations.

Port Due

Port dues, also known as harbor dues or port charges, are fees levied by port authorities on ships, vessels, or cargo for the use of a port facility and its services. These charges help fund the maintenance, development, and operational costs of ports and harbors. Port dues are common at both commercial and public ports worldwide and are an integral part of maritime logistics and trade. Here are key points about port dues:

1. **Purpose:** The primary purpose of port dues is to cover the expenses associated with maintaining and operating port infrastructure, ensuring navigational safety, providing pilotage services, and managing various port facilities and services.
2. **Calculation:** Port dues are typically calculated based on several factors, including the type and size of the vessel, the duration of stay in the port, the type and quantity of cargo, and the services utilized. Different ports may have varying fee structures.
3. **Vessel Types:** Different types of vessels, such as container ships, bulk carriers, tankers, and passenger liners, may incur varying port dues based on their tonnage, length overall (LOA), and other characteristics.
4. **Cargo Handling:** Some port dues are directly related to cargo handling, and charges may be based on the volume or weight of cargo loaded or unloaded at the port.
5. **Berthage Fees:** These fees are associated with using a berth or quay within the port. Berthage charges are calculated based on the vessel's size and the duration of mooring.
6. **Tonnage Dues:** Tonnage dues are based on the tonnage of the vessel, typically measured in gross registered tons (GRT) or net registered tons (NRT).
7. **Pilotage Fees:** Pilotage services involve the guidance of vessels into and out of the port, especially in narrow or challenging navigation areas. Pilotage fees are separate charges and may be assessed based on vessel tonnage.
8. **Navigational Aids:** Port dues often contribute to the maintenance and operation of navigational aids, such as

lighthouses, buoys, and beacons, which enhance safety for vessels entering and exiting the port.

9. **Environmental Fees:** Some ports levy additional charges to fund environmental initiatives, such as pollution control and waste disposal.
10. **Customs and Security:** In some cases, port dues may include customs or security fees associated with cargo inspections and security measures.
11. **Revenue for Port Authorities:** Port dues represent a significant source of revenue for port authorities, enabling them to invest in infrastructure improvements, expand capacity, and enhance the efficiency of port operations.
12. **Regulations and Collection:** Port dues are subject to local regulations and collection procedures, and they may vary from one port to another and from country to country.
13. **Payment:** Vessel owners, operators, and cargo owners are responsible for paying port dues. These fees are typically settled through port agents or directly with the port authority.

Port dues are an essential aspect of maritime commerce and play a critical role in ensuring the sustainability and functionality of ports and harbors, which, in turn, support global trade and transportation networks. They are an integral part of the cost structure for shipping companies and businesses involved in international trade.

Light house due clearing certificate

A Light House Due Clearing Certificate is a document issued by a port or maritime authority to confirm that the applicable light dues, or fees, have been paid for a particular vessel. These dues are collected to fund the operation, maintenance, and construction of lighthouses and other navigational aids that enhance maritime safety. Here are key points about the Light House Due Clearing Certificate:

1. **Purpose:** The primary purpose of the Light House Due Clearing Certificate is to provide evidence that the required light dues have been paid for a specific vessel, allowing it to navigate and access ports and waterways with the assistance of lighthouses and other navigational aids.
2. **Light Dues:** Light dues are charges assessed on vessels, primarily based on their tonnage, as a contribution to the cost of operating and maintaining lighthouses, buoys, beacons, and other aids to navigation.
3. **Calculation:** Light dues are typically calculated based on a vessel's tonnage, which may be measured in gross registered tons (GRT) or other tonnage measurements as specified by local regulations.
4. **Collection:** The collection of light dues and the issuance of the Light House Due Clearing Certificate are usually the responsibility of the relevant port authority or maritime agency.
5. **Proof of Payment:** The Light House Due Clearing Certificate serves as proof that the vessel has paid the required light dues and is compliant with the regulations governing the use of navigational aids. It is presented to port authorities and customs officials as part of the vessel's documentation.
6. **Navigational Aid Funding:** The revenue generated from light dues is crucial for the continued operation, maintenance, and improvement of navigational aids that enhance the safety of maritime navigation, especially in areas with challenging or hazardous waters.
7. **Validity Period:** The certificate may have a specified validity period, after which it must be renewed by paying the appropriate light dues for continued access to ports and navigation services.
8. **Compliance with Regulations:** Compliance with light dues

and possession of the Light House Due Clearing Certificate are typically required by international maritime regulations and local port regulations. Non-compliance can result in delays and fines.

9. **Global Application:** Light dues and the requirement for the Light House Due Clearing Certificate are not limited to a specific region or country. They are applicable in many maritime nations to support safe navigation.
10. **Enforcement:** Port authorities and customs officials may verify the validity of the certificate during vessel inspections or when granting access to ports and waterways. Compliance checks ensure that vessels contribute to the cost of maintaining navigational safety.

In summary, the Light House Due Clearing Certificate is a document that confirms the payment of light dues by a vessel, allowing it to navigate safely and access ports and waterways with the assistance of lighthouses and other navigational aids. It is a key element in maritime safety and regulatory compliance.

Cargo information documents

Cargo information documents are essential paperwork used in the shipping and logistics industry to provide comprehensive information about the goods being transported. These documents are crucial for ensuring the proper handling, tracking, and customs clearance of cargo throughout its journey from the point of origin to the final destination. Here are some of the key cargo information documents:

1. **Packing List:**
    - A packing list is a detailed document that itemizes the contents of each package or container within a shipment. It typically includes information such as

the product description, quantity, weight, dimensions, and packaging materials used.

2. **Bill of Lading (B/L):**
   - The Bill of Lading is a multi-purpose document that serves as a receipt for cargo, a contract of carriage, and a title document. It contains essential information about the shipment, including details about the shipper, consignee, description of goods, weight, and destination.
3. **Commercial Invoice:**
   - A commercial invoice is a sales document issued by the seller to the buyer, providing detailed information about the goods, their value, payment terms, and shipping terms. It is used for customs clearance and as evidence of the commercial transaction.
4. **Certificate of Origin:**
   - This document certifies the country of origin of the goods being shipped. It may be required for customs purposes, trade agreements, or tariff classification.
5. **Dangerous Goods Declaration (IMO Declaration):**
   - When shipping hazardous materials or dangerous goods, a dangerous goods declaration is mandatory. It provides essential information about the nature of the hazardous goods, their classification, and safety precautions.
6. **Weight Certificate:**
   - A weight certificate confirms the weight of the cargo, which is particularly important for calculating shipping costs and ensuring safe loading on vessels or aircraft.
7. **Freight Booking Confirmation:**

    - This document provides information about the booking of cargo space, including the carrier, vessel or flight details, and scheduled departure and arrival dates. It is used for tracking and coordination.
8. **Insurance Certificate (Marine Insurance Policy):**
    - An insurance certificate or marine insurance policy confirms that the cargo is insured during transit. It outlines the terms, conditions, and coverage limits of the insurance.
9. **Customs Declaration:**
    - Customs declarations are mandatory documents that provide information about the cargo's value, origin, and other relevant details. They are used to assess import duties and taxes and to ensure compliance with customs regulations.
10. **Shipment Tracking Information:**
    - Shipment tracking information, often provided electronically, allows for real-time tracking of the cargo's location and status throughout its journey.
11. **Certificates of Inspection:**
    - In some cases, certificates of inspection are required to verify the quality, condition, or safety compliance of specific goods.
12. **Phytosanitary Certificate:**
    - This certificate is issued to confirm that plant products meet the required phytosanitary standards and are free from pests and diseases.

These cargo information documents play a critical role in ensuring the smooth flow of goods through the supply chain, from the point of origin to the final destination. They facilitate customs clearance, help mitigate risks, and provide accurate and detailed information to all parties involved in the shipping and logistics process. Properly completing and presenting these documents is essential for efficient and compliant cargo handling and transportation.

Dutiable, Non dutiable list

"Dutiable" and "non-dutiable" refer to the classification of goods based on whether they are subject to import duties or taxes when crossing international borders. These terms are important for customs and trade regulations. Here's what they mean:

Dutiable Goods:

- Dutiable goods are products or items that are subject to import duties, taxes, or tariffs when they enter a country. These charges are imposed by the customs authorities of the importing country.
- Import duties are typically calculated based on the customs valuation of the goods, which includes factors like the product's value, origin, and classification.
- Duties are designed to generate revenue for the government, protect domestic industries, and regulate the flow of goods across borders.
- Examples of dutiable goods may include certain types of textiles, electronics, luxury goods, and alcoholic beverages.

Non-Dutiable Goods:

- Non-dutiable goods, on the other hand, are products that are exempt from import duties or taxes when they enter a country. They are often considered essential items, raw materials, or goods that have special trade agreements or preferential treatment.
- Governments may exempt specific goods from duties to promote certain industries, support humanitarian efforts, or encourage international trade.

- Examples of non-dutiable goods may include basic foodstuffs, medical supplies, humanitarian aid, and some raw materials used for domestic production.

It's important to note that the classification of goods as dutiable or non-dutiable can vary from one country to another and may change over time due to changes in trade policies, regulations, and international agreements. Importers and exporters must be aware of these classifications and adhere to customs regulations to ensure the proper and legal movement of goods across borders. Violating customs regulations can result in fines, penalties, or confiscation of goods.

Crew qualification certificate

A Crew Qualification Certificate, often referred to as a Seafarer's Certificate or Maritime Qualification Certificate, is an official document issued to individuals working in the maritime industry. This certificate serves as evidence of a person's qualifications, training, and competence to perform specific roles and duties on board a ship or vessel. Here are key points about the Crew Qualification Certificate:

Purpose:

- The primary purpose of a Crew Qualification Certificate is to verify that an individual has met the required standards, undergone necessary training, and possesses the necessary skills and knowledge to work safely and effectively in the maritime sector.

Issuing Authority:

- These certificates are typically issued by the maritime authority or regulatory body of the flag state or country where the individual is registered as a seafarer.

Types of Certificates:

- Crew Qualification Certificates come in various types and levels, depending on the specific role and responsibilities of the seafarer. Common types include:
    1. **Deck Officer's Certificate:** Issued to individuals who serve as navigational officers or masters (captains) of a vessel.
    2. **Engineer Officer's Certificate:** Issued to individuals responsible for the operation and maintenance of a vessel's engines and machinery.
    3. **Ratings Certificate:** Issued to individuals in support roles, such as deckhands, able seamen, or engine room personnel.
    4. **STCW Certificates:** In accordance with the International Convention on Standards of Training, Certification, and Watchkeeping for Seafarers (STCW), certain positions require STCW certificates, which are internationally recognized.

Training and Qualifications:

- To obtain a Crew Qualification Certificate, individuals typically must complete specific training programs, accumulate sea service hours, and pass examinations. The training covers various aspects, including safety, navigation, vessel operations, and emergency response.

Renewal and Upkeep:

- Crew Qualification Certificates are subject to renewal at regular intervals to ensure that seafarers maintain their competency and stay updated with changes in regulations and technology.

Legal Requirement:

- In many countries, working on a ship without a valid Crew Qualification Certificate is illegal and can result in penalties or fines.

International Recognition:

- Many Crew Qualification Certificates, especially those issued in accordance with STCW, are recognized internationally. Seafarers can use these certificates to work on vessels registered in different countries.

Safety and Competence:

- These certificates are essential for ensuring the safety of crew members, passengers, and vessels at sea. They demonstrate that seafarers are trained to respond effectively to emergencies and operate vessels professionally.

Career Advancement:

- Crew Qualification Certificates also play a crucial role in seafarers' career advancement. Higher-level certificates open up opportunities for more responsible roles and increased responsibilities on board.

Overall, Crew Qualification Certificates are critical documents that demonstrate a seafarer's competency and qualifications, ensuring the safe and efficient operation of ships and vessels in the maritime industry. They are a testament to a seafarer's commitment to professionalism and safety at sea.

List of life saving appliances certificate

and Dry docking certificate

Life-Saving Appliances Certificate and Dry Docking Certificate are crucial documents in the maritime industry, both related to the safety and maintenance of vessels. Here's what each of these certificates entails:

Life-Saving Appliances Certificate:

- The Life-Saving Appliances Certificate, often referred to as a Lifeboat Certificate, is issued to vessels to confirm that their life-saving equipment and appliances comply with international maritime safety regulations. These appliances are essential for ensuring the safety and survival of crew members and passengers in emergency situations at sea. Key aspects of this certificate include:
    1. **Inspection and Compliance:** The certificate verifies that the vessel's life-saving equipment, such as lifeboats, life rafts, lifebuoys, life jackets, and associated launching and recovery systems, has been inspected, tested, and found to be in compliance with safety standards, often established by organizations like the International Maritime Organization (IMO).
    2. **Validity:** The Life-Saving Appliances Certificate is typically issued for a specified period, and it must be renewed through regular inspections and maintenance to ensure that the equipment remains in working order and ready for use in emergencies.
    3. **Safety Drills:** Vessel crews are required to conduct regular safety drills to demonstrate their proficiency in using the life-saving equipment. The certificate may include records of these drills.

Dry Docking Certificate:

- A Dry Docking Certificate, also known as a Certificate of Dry Docking, is issued to vessels after they have undergone a dry docking process. Dry docking involves taking a vessel out of the water for inspection, maintenance, and repair. This certificate is essential for confirming that the vessel is in seaworthy condition and complies with safety and environmental regulations. Key aspects of this certificate include:
    1. **Dry Docking Schedule:** The certificate typically indicates the date and location of the dry docking, outlining when and where the inspection and maintenance took place.
    2. **Inspection and Repairs:** It confirms that the vessel underwent a thorough inspection during dry docking and that any necessary repairs, maintenance, and modifications were completed to ensure the vessel's safety and compliance with regulations.
    3. **Condition and Compliance:** The certificate affirms that the vessel is in a suitable condition to return to service, meets safety standards, and complies with international maritime regulations.
    4. **Validity:** Dry Docking Certificates are typically issued for a specific duration, after which the vessel must undergo another dry docking process to ensure continued seaworthiness.

These certificates are crucial for demonstrating that vessels are equipped with functional life-saving appliances and are well-maintained through dry docking processes, contributing to the safety of crew members, passengers, and the maritime environment. Compliance with these requirements is mandatory for vessels operating under international maritime regulations.

Classification societies certificate

A Classification Society Certificate, often referred to as a Class Certificate, is an official document issued by a classification society to a vessel that certifies that the ship meets certain standards of design, construction, maintenance, and safety. Classification societies are independent organizations that provide services related to the inspection and classification of ships to ensure their seaworthiness and compliance with international maritime regulations. Here are key points about Classification Society Certificates:

Purpose:

- The primary purpose of a Classification Society Certificate is to confirm that a ship has been built, maintained, and operated in accordance with the rules and standards established by the classification society.

Classification Societies:

- There are several major classification societies worldwide, including the American Bureau of Shipping (ABS), Lloyd's Register (LR), DNV GL, Bureau Veritas (BV), and others. Each society has its own set of rules and standards.

Inspection and Classification:

- Before a vessel is granted a Classification Society Certificate, it undergoes a series of inspections and surveys by qualified surveyors from the classification society. These surveys cover various aspects of the ship's design, construction, and maintenance.

Types of Certificates:

- Classification Society Certificates come in various types and are often specific to different aspects of the vessel. Common types include:
    1. **Hull Certificate:** Certifies that the ship's hull is constructed and maintained to class standards.
    2. **Machinery Certificate:** Certifies the ship's machinery, including engines and propulsion systems.
    3. **Safety Equipment Certificate:** Certifies that safety equipment and systems on board meet required standards.
    4. **Load Line Certificate:** Certifies compliance with load line regulations to ensure the vessel's stability and safety.
    5. **International Maritime Organization (IMO) Certificates:** These may include certificates related to the International Convention for the Safety of Life at Sea (SOLAS), International Convention for the Prevention of Pollution from Ships (MARPOL), and others.

Validity and Renewal:

- Classification Society Certificates have specified validity periods, and they must be renewed through periodic surveys and inspections to ensure that the ship continues to meet class standards.

Regulatory Compliance:

- Classification Society Certificates are often required for vessels to operate legally and enter ports worldwide. They demonstrate that a vessel is in compliance with international and national maritime regulations.

Insurance and Financing:

- Classification Society Certificates may be required by insurers and financial institutions when providing coverage or financing for ships. These certificates offer assurance that the vessel is well-maintained and less likely to be involved in accidents or incidents.

Safety and Quality Assurance:

- By adhering to the standards set by classification societies, vessels are more likely to operate safely, efficiently, and with reduced environmental impact.

Public Record:

- The status of a vessel's Class Certificate is a matter of public record and can be accessed by interested parties, including shipowners, charterers, and port authorities.

In summary, Classification Society Certificates play a crucial role in ensuring the seaworthiness, safety, and compliance of vessels with established maritime standards and regulations. They provide assurance to shipowners, operators, and the maritime community that vessels are constructed and maintained to the highest quality and safety standards.

Stability booklet

A Stability Booklet, also known as a Stability Manual or Stability Book, is an essential document on board a ship that provides critical information about the vessel's stability characteristics, guidelines for safe operation, and procedures to ensure the ship's stability under various conditions. This booklet is crucial for the safety of the vessel, crew, passengers, and cargo. Here are key points about the Stability Booklet:

Purpose:

- The primary purpose of a Stability Booklet is to ensure the safe and stable operation of the ship under different conditions, including during loading, unloading, and while at sea.

Stability Information:

- The booklet contains detailed stability data and information about the ship's stability characteristics, such as its metacentric height (GM), righting levers, and stability curves. These data help assess the ship's stability under various conditions.

Loading and Ballasting Instructions:

- It provides guidelines for the proper loading and ballasting of the vessel to maintain adequate stability. This includes information on the distribution of cargo, ballast water management, and the use of ballast tanks.

Operational Limits:

- The Stability Booklet specifies operational limits, such as maximum permissible drafts, angles of heel, and load line restrictions, to ensure the ship remains within safe stability parameters.

Emergency Procedures:

- In case of emergencies, the booklet may include procedures to respond to stability-threatening situations, such as flooding, shifting cargo, or damage to the vessel. This information is critical for the crew's response during emergencies.

Regulatory Compliance:

- Ships are required to carry a Stability Booklet to comply with international maritime regulations, including those outlined in the International Maritime Organization (IMO) regulations, such as the International Convention for the Safety of Life at Sea (SOLAS).

Ship-Specific Data:

- The Stability Booklet is ship-specific and is tailored to the vessel's design, size, and stability characteristics. It reflects the results of stability assessments and calculations conducted during the ship's design and construction phase.

Accessibility:

- The Stability Booklet must be readily accessible to the ship's master, officers, and crew at all times, particularly when making critical decisions related to cargo loading, ballasting, and navigation.

Training:

- Crew members, particularly officers responsible for cargo handling and stability, receive training on how to use the Stability Booklet effectively and ensure safe ship operations.

Amendments and Updates:

- Over time, changes in the ship's configuration, equipment, or weight distribution may necessitate updates to the Stability Booklet to ensure its accuracy and relevance.

In summary, the Stability Booklet is a vital reference document that supports safe and efficient maritime operations. It plays a central role in maintaining a ship's stability, preventing accidents, and ensuring compliance with international safety standards. The use of this booklet is essential for the safe transportation of cargo and passengers at sea.

Certificate of inspection of goods

A Certificate of Inspection of Goods, commonly known as a Cargo Inspection Certificate, is an official document issued after a cargo inspection has been conducted. This inspection aims to verify the quantity, quality, condition, and compliance of goods with relevant standards, regulations, and contractual agreements. Here are key points about the Certificate of Inspection of Goods:

Purpose:

- The primary purpose of a Cargo Inspection Certificate is to provide an independent and objective assessment of the goods being shipped. It verifies that the goods meet specified criteria and are in suitable condition for transportation.

Types of Inspection:

- Cargo inspections can encompass various aspects, including:
    1. **Quantity Inspection:** Verifying the quantity of goods shipped to match the quantity specified in contracts or shipping documents.
    2. **Quality Inspection:** Assessing the quality of goods, including their specifications, characteristics, and compliance with applicable standards.
    3. **Condition Inspection:** Examining the condition of

goods, including any damage or deterioration that may have occurred during storage or handling.

4. **Weight Inspection:** Confirming the weight of goods to ensure accuracy in accordance with trade agreements or shipping contracts.
5. **Chemical Analysis:** Conducting chemical tests and analysis on certain types of cargo, such as chemicals or hazardous materials, to ensure safety and compliance with regulations.

Issuing Authority:

- The Certificate of Inspection of Goods is typically issued by an independent inspection agency or authority that specializes in cargo inspection. These agencies are responsible for conducting impartial assessments.

Contents:

- The certificate includes detailed information about the inspection, such as the type of inspection performed, the date and location of the inspection, the identity of the inspector, a description of the goods, and the results of the inspection.

Compliance and Certification:

- If the goods meet the specified criteria and standards, the certificate will certify that the cargo is compliant and suitable for shipment.

Non-Compliance and Exceptions:

- If any discrepancies, defects, or non-compliance issues are identified during the inspection, they will be noted on the certificate, and appropriate action may be recommended, such as rejection, remediation, or re-inspection.

Legal and Contractual Implications:

- Cargo Inspection Certificates can have significant legal and contractual implications. They serve as evidence of the cargo's condition and compliance, protecting the interests of both the shipper and the recipient.

Trade and Customs Clearance:

- In many cases, customs authorities and trade partners may require a Cargo Inspection Certificate as part of the documentation required for customs clearance and trade compliance.

Dispute Resolution:

- In the event of disputes or disagreements regarding the condition or quality of goods, the Certificate of Inspection of Goods can serve as a crucial piece of evidence in resolving such disputes.

In summary, a Certificate of Inspection of Goods is a vital document that provides assurance about the quality, quantity, and condition of goods being shipped. It helps facilitate trade, ensures compliance with regulations and contractual agreements, and contributes to transparency and trust in international commerce.

Documents for marine loss insurance claim.

When filing a marine loss insurance claim, it's essential to provide thorough documentation to support your claim and facilitate the claims process. The specific documents required may vary depending on the circumstances of the loss and your insurance policy, but here is a list of common documents typically needed for a marine loss insurance claim:

1. **Marine Insurance Policy:** Provide a copy of your marine insurance policy, including all relevant endorsements and amendments.
2. **Claim Form:** Complete the insurance company's claim form accurately, providing all requested information.
3. **Notice of Loss:** Notify your insurance company promptly of the loss, typically within the timeframe specified in your policy. Include details such as the date, time, location, and nature of the loss.
4. **Certificate of Insurance:** Provide a copy of the certificate of insurance that outlines the coverage in effect at the time of the loss.
5. **Vessel Information:** If the loss involves a vessel, provide detailed information about the vessel, including its name, registration number, type, specifications, and ownership details.
6. **Incident Report:** Prepare a comprehensive incident report that describes the circumstances of the loss, including the cause, extent of damage, and any contributing factors. Include photographs and diagrams if applicable.
7. **Cargo Details:** If the loss involves cargo, provide information about the cargo, such as its description, quantity, value,

packaging, and shipping documents (bills of lading, invoices, packing lists).

8. **Survey Report:** If a surveyor assessed the damage or loss, provide a copy of the survey report. The report should include findings, recommendations, and any supporting evidence.
9. **Evidence of Loss:** Include any evidence that supports your claim, such as photographs, videos, witness statements, or expert opinions.
10. **Repair Estimates:** If the loss involves damage to a vessel or cargo, obtain repair estimates from qualified professionals or repair facilities.
11. **Police or Incident Reports:** If the loss resulted from criminal activity or another incident that required police involvement, provide copies of police reports and incident reports.
12. **Communication Records:** Include any correspondence, emails, or communication logs related to the incident, including communications with third parties involved in the loss.
13. **Bills and Invoices:** If you incurred expenses related to mitigating the loss, include copies of bills, invoices, and receipts for services rendered or repairs made.
14. **Witness Statements:** If there were witnesses to the loss, obtain their statements and contact information to support your claim.
15. **Legal Documents:** If legal proceedings or disputes are involved, provide copies of relevant legal documents, including court orders, judgments, or settlements.
16. **Customs and Port Records:** Include customs clearance documents and port records, especially if the loss occurred during shipping or transportation.
17. **Subrogation Rights:** If your insurer intends to pursue subrogation (seeking recovery from responsible parties),

provide any information or documentation required to support this process.

18. **Any Other Relevant Documentation:** Include any additional documents or information that may be relevant to your claim.

It's crucial to work closely with your insurance company's claims adjuster or representative to ensure that you provide all necessary documentation and meet any specific requirements outlined in your policy. Timely and accurate submission of documents can expedite the claims process and help you receive a fair and timely settlement for your marine loss insurance claim.

Chapter-5 Documents with in the Organisation

Documents within an organization refer to the various types of paperwork, records, files, and digital documents that are generated, maintained, and used for administrative, operational, and informational purposes. These documents play a crucial role in the functioning of an organization, and they can vary widely depending on the type and size of the organization. Here are some common types of documents within an organization:

1. **Business Plans:** Documents outlining the organization's strategic goals, objectives, and plans for growth and development.
2. **Financial Documents:** Including income statements, balance sheets, budgets, financial reports, and expense records.
3. **Human Resources Documents:** Such as employee contracts, resumes, performance reviews, and personnel files.
4. **Legal Documents:** Including contracts, agreements, permits, licenses, and compliance records.
5. **Policies and Procedures Manuals:** Detailing the organization's policies, rules, and procedures for employees and operations.
6. **Meeting Minutes:** Records of discussions, decisions, and actions taken during organizational meetings.
7. **Project Plans:** Documents outlining project goals, schedules, tasks, and resource allocation.
8. **Marketing and Sales Materials:** Such as marketing plans, advertisements, brochures, and sales reports.
9. **Customer Records:** Including customer profiles, purchase histories, and contact information.
10. **Vendor and Supplier Agreements:** Contracts and documents related to agreements with suppliers and vendors.
11. **Inventory Records:** Records of stock levels, stock movements, and inventory management.

12. **Quality Control and Assurance Records:** Documents related to quality standards, testing, and product/service quality.
13. **Health and Safety Records:** Documents outlining safety protocols, incident reports, and safety inspections.
14. **Training Materials:** Materials used for employee training and development.
15. **Organizational Charts:** Visual representations of the company's structure and hierarchy.
16. **Emails and Correspondence:** Digital and physical correspondence within and outside the organization.
17. **Strategic Plans:** Long-term plans and visions for the organization's future.
18. **Technical Documentation:** Manuals, schematics, and technical specifications for products and systems.
19. **Customer Feedback and Surveys:** Records of customer feedback, satisfaction surveys, and complaints.
20. **Research Reports:** Findings from market research, industry analysis, and internal research efforts.
21. **Invoices and Receipts:** Documents related to financial transactions, payments, and receipts.
22. **Intellectual Property Records:** Patents, trademarks, copyrights, and other intellectual property documentation.
23. **IT and Data Records:** Documents related to IT infrastructure, data management, and cybersecurity.
24. **Emergency and Disaster Plans:** Documents outlining procedures for responding to emergencies and disasters.
25. **Employee Handbooks:** Guides containing information on company policies, benefits, and expectations for employees.

Effective document management and organization are essential for maintaining transparency, compliance, and efficiency within an organization. Properly stored and accessible documents help facilitate decision-making, enhance communication, and support various business processes. Many organizations also use document management software and systems to streamline document handling and retrieval.

Truck maintenance certificate

A Truck Maintenance Certificate is an official document that provides evidence that a commercial truck or fleet of trucks has undergone regular maintenance and inspections, ensuring their roadworthiness and compliance with safety regulations. This certificate is an essential part of fleet management and compliance with transportation industry standards. Here are key points about the Truck Maintenance Certificate:

Purpose:

- The primary purpose of a Truck Maintenance Certificate is to verify that a truck has been properly maintained and is in good working condition. It is often required to comply with legal and safety regulations.

Issuing Authority:

- The certificate is typically issued by the owner or operator of the commercial truck, the trucking company, or a maintenance facility responsible for servicing the vehicles.

Maintenance Records:

- The certificate includes detailed maintenance records, indicating the dates of maintenance activities, types of maintenance performed (e.g., routine inspections, oil changes, brake repairs), and the names of mechanics or technicians who conducted the maintenance.

Inspection Results:

- It may include the results of safety inspections, emissions testing, or other regulatory checks required by local, state, or federal authorities.

Vehicle Information:

- The certificate contains detailed information about the truck, such as its make, model, registration number, vehicle identification number (VIN), and other identifying details.

Safety Compliance:

- The certificate confirms that the truck meets safety and environmental compliance standards, including adherence to regulations set forth by the Department of Transportation (DOT) in the United States or similar agencies in other countries.

Expiration Date:

- Truck Maintenance Certificates typically have an expiration date, after which the vehicle is required to undergo another round of inspections and maintenance to renew the certificate.

Legal Requirement:

- Many jurisdictions require commercial trucks to have valid Maintenance Certificates to operate legally on public roads. Failure to maintain a certificate can result in fines, penalties, or the suspension of the truck's operating privileges.

Insurance Requirement:

- Some insurance providers may require proof of regular maintenance as a condition for providing coverage, particularly for commercial trucking companies.

Fleet Management:

- For organizations with multiple trucks, maintaining a record of Truck Maintenance Certificates is essential for fleet management, tracking maintenance schedules, and ensuring compliance.

Safety and Reliability:

- Regular maintenance and the associated certificates contribute to the safety and reliability of trucks, reducing the risk of accidents and breakdowns on the road.

Audits and Inspections:

- Regulatory authorities, insurance companies, and auditors may request Truck Maintenance Certificates as part of compliance checks, audits, or investigations.

Truck Maintenance Certificates play a significant role in ensuring that commercial trucks are safe to operate and meet regulatory requirements. They provide documentation of ongoing maintenance efforts, which is crucial for both road safety and the continued operation of the commercial trucking industry.

Warehousing safety certificate

A Warehousing Safety Certificate is an official document that signifies that a warehouse facility has met specific safety standards and compliance requirements. It demonstrates that the warehouse is committed to ensuring the safety of its employees, visitors, and the goods stored within the facility. Here are key points about the Warehousing Safety Certificate:

Purpose:

- The primary purpose of a Warehousing Safety Certificate is to provide evidence that a warehouse facility is safe and compliant with safety regulations. It promotes a culture of safety and reduces the risk of accidents and injuries within the warehouse.

Issuing Authority:

- Typically, the certificate is issued by regulatory agencies, government authorities, or industry-specific organizations responsible for overseeing warehouse safety standards and compliance.

Safety Standards and Compliance:

- To obtain a Warehousing Safety Certificate, a warehouse must demonstrate that it complies with specific safety standards and regulations. These standards often include fire safety, electrical safety, structural safety, material handling equipment safety, and more.

Safety Policies and Procedures:

- The certificate may require the warehouse to have documented safety policies and procedures in place, including emergency response plans, safety training programs, and regular safety inspections.

Safety Training:

- It may require warehouse personnel to undergo safety training programs to ensure they are aware of safety protocols, hazard identification, and emergency procedures.

Regular Inspections:

- Warehouses seeking certification often undergo regular safety inspections conducted by authorized inspectors to verify compliance with safety standards.

Emergency Preparedness:

- The certificate may require the warehouse to have adequate emergency equipment and procedures in place, such as fire extinguishers, sprinkler systems, emergency exits, and first-aid supplies.

Material Handling Equipment:

- Certification may include checks for the safety of material handling equipment, such as forklifts and conveyor systems.

Occupational Health and Safety:

- Warehouses may need to demonstrate their commitment to occupational health and safety standards, including measures to prevent workplace injuries and illnesses.

Environmental Compliance:

- Some warehousing safety certifications also consider environmental factors, such as hazardous material handling, waste disposal, and environmental impact assessments.

Validity and Renewal:

- Warehousing Safety Certificates typically have a validity period, after which the warehouse must undergo recertification to ensure ongoing safety compliance.

Liability and Insurance:

- Having a Warehousing Safety Certificate may impact insurance coverage, as insurers may offer better rates or conditions to facilities that meet safety standards.

Customer and Partner Assurance:

- For warehousing companies, having a safety certificate can serve as a competitive advantage by assuring customers and partners that their goods will be stored in a safe and secure environment.

In summary, a Warehousing Safety Certificate is a valuable credential that demonstrates a commitment to safety and compliance within a warehouse facility. It promotes a safer working environment, reduces the risk of accidents, and enhances the overall reputation and credibility of the facility.

Warehousing material handling equipment safety certificate

A Warehousing Material Handling Equipment Safety Certificate is an official document that confirms that the material handling equipment used within a warehouse facility complies with safety standards and regulations. It signifies that the equipment has undergone inspections, maintenance, and training to ensure the safety of workers, visitors, and the efficient operation of the warehouse. Here are key points about the Warehousing Material Handling Equipment Safety Certificate:

Purpose:

- The primary purpose of this certificate is to provide assurance that material handling equipment within a warehouse is safe, properly maintained, and compliant with safety regulations. It helps prevent accidents and injuries related to equipment operation.

Issuing Authority:

- Warehousing Material Handling Equipment Safety Certificates are typically issued by regulatory agencies, government authorities, or industry-specific organizations responsible for overseeing safety standards for such equipment.

Types of Equipment:

- This certificate may cover various types of material handling equipment used in warehouses, including forklifts, pallet jacks, conveyor systems, hoists, cranes, and automated guided vehicles (AGVs), among others.

Safety Standards and Compliance:

- To obtain the certificate, the warehouse must demonstrate that its material handling equipment adheres to specific safety standards and regulations. These standards often include equipment design, maintenance, operator training, and safe operating practices.

Equipment Inspections:

- Warehouses seeking certification are typically required to conduct regular inspections of material handling equipment to ensure that it is in safe working condition. These inspections may be performed by certified inspectors or internal maintenance teams.

Maintenance Records:

- The certificate may require the warehouse to maintain detailed records of equipment maintenance and repairs, including records of inspections, servicing, and replacement of parts.

Operator Training:

- Safety certificates often include provisions for the training of equipment operators to ensure that they are knowledgeable about equipment operation, safety procedures, and hazard awareness.

Safe Operating Practices:

- Warehouses must demonstrate that they promote and enforce

safe operating practices for material handling equipment, which may include speed limits, load capacity restrictions, and guidelines for avoiding accidents.

Emergency Procedures:

- The certificate may require the warehouse to have documented emergency procedures in place for dealing with equipment-related accidents or malfunctions.

Renewal and Recertification:

- Warehousing Material Handling Equipment Safety Certificates typically have an expiration date, and warehouses must undergo recertification to ensure continued safety compliance.

Liability and Insurance:

- Having a valid certificate can impact insurance coverage, as insurers may consider it a positive factor when providing coverage for potential equipment-related accidents.

Customer Assurance:

- For warehousing companies, holding this certificate can provide assurance to customers that their goods will be handled and stored with a strong emphasis on safety and risk mitigation.

In summary, a Warehousing Material Handling Equipment Safety Certificate is a critical document that confirms that material handling equipment within a warehouse facility meets safety standards and is maintained for safe operation. It plays a vital role in preventing accidents, ensuring worker safety, and maintaining the efficiency and reliability of warehouse operations.

Rail goods wagon safety maintenance certificates

A Rail Goods Wagon Safety Maintenance Certificate is an official document that confirms that a rail goods wagon (also known as a railcar or freight car) has undergone regular maintenance and inspections to ensure its safe and efficient operation on rail networks. These certificates are crucial for railway operators, owners, and regulatory authorities to ensure the safety and compliance of rail freight transportation. Here are key points about Rail Goods Wagon Safety Maintenance Certificates:

Purpose:

- The primary purpose of a Rail Goods Wagon Safety Maintenance Certificate is to provide evidence that a railcar has been properly maintained and is in compliance with safety and maintenance regulations. It is essential to promote railway safety and reduce the risk of accidents.

Issuing Authority:

- Typically, these certificates are issued by railway authorities, regulatory agencies, or organizations responsible for overseeing rail safety standards and compliance.

Maintenance Standards and Compliance:

- To obtain a Rail Goods Wagon Safety Maintenance Certificate, the railcar must demonstrate compliance with specific maintenance and safety standards. These standards cover various aspects of railcar maintenance, including structural integrity, braking systems, wheel and axle condition, and safety equipment.

Inspections and Maintenance Records:

- Railway operators and owners are required to maintain comprehensive records of inspections, maintenance activities, and repairs performed on rail goods wagons. These records provide evidence of compliance with maintenance standards.

Frequency of Inspections:

- The certificate may specify the frequency of inspections and maintenance activities, which may include routine inspections, intermediate inspections, and major overhauls, depending on the age and usage of the railcar.

Safety Equipment:

- Rail goods wagons must be equipped with appropriate safety features, including hand brakes, automatic brakes, safety couplers, and emergency braking systems. The certificate may require verification of the functionality of these safety components.

Operator Training:

- Certificates may include requirements for the training and certification of railcar operators to ensure safe handling and operation of the equipment.

Emergency Procedures:

- The certificate may require railway operators to have documented emergency procedures in place for addressing accidents, derailments, or other safety incidents involving rail goods wagons.

Environmental Compliance:

- Some certificates may also consider environmental factors, such as hazardous cargo transport, waste disposal, and measures to prevent spills or contamination.

Validity and Renewal:

- Rail Goods Wagon Safety Maintenance Certificates typically have a validity period, after which the railcar must undergo another round of inspections and maintenance to renew the certificate.

Liability and Insurance:

- Holding a valid certificate can impact insurance coverage, as insurers may consider it a positive factor when providing coverage for potential railcar-related incidents.

Regulatory Compliance:

- These certificates are essential to demonstrate compliance with railway regulations and safety standards established by national and international authorities.

In summary, a Rail Goods Wagon Safety Maintenance Certificate is a critical document that ensures the safe and reliable operation of rail goods wagons in the transportation of freight. It plays a vital role in rail safety, regulatory compliance, and the prevention of accidents on rail networks.

Air Cargo maintenance certificate

An Air Cargo Maintenance Certificate is an official document that certifies that an aircraft used for the transport of air cargo has undergone regular maintenance and inspections to ensure its safe and reliable operation. These certificates are essential for airlines, cargo operators, and aviation regulatory authorities to ensure the safety and compliance of air cargo transportation. Here are key points about the Air Cargo Maintenance Certificate:

Purpose:

- The primary purpose of an Air Cargo Maintenance Certificate is to provide evidence that an aircraft dedicated to air cargo operations has been properly maintained and is in compliance with aviation safety and maintenance regulations. It is crucial for promoting aviation safety and reducing the risk of accidents.

Issuing Authority:

- Typically, Air Cargo Maintenance Certificates are issued by civil aviation authorities, regulatory agencies, or organizations responsible for overseeing aviation safety standards and compliance.

Maintenance Standards and Compliance:

- To obtain an Air Cargo Maintenance Certificate, the aircraft must demonstrate compliance with specific maintenance and safety standards. These standards cover various aspects of aircraft maintenance, including airframe integrity, propulsion systems, avionics, safety equipment, and cargo handling systems.

Inspections and Maintenance Records:

- Airlines and cargo operators are required to maintain comprehensive records of inspections, maintenance activities, and repairs performed on cargo aircraft. These records provide evidence of compliance with maintenance standards.

Frequency of Inspections:

- The certificate may specify the frequency of inspections and maintenance activities, which may include routine inspections, major checks (such as A-checks and C-checks), and component replacements based on flight hours and cycles.

Safety Equipment:

- Cargo aircraft must be equipped with appropriate safety features, including fire suppression systems, cargo restraints, smoke detection systems, and emergency exits. The certificate may require verification of the functionality of these safety components.

Cargo Handling Procedures:

- Certificates may include requirements for cargo handling procedures, including the secure loading and unloading of cargo, weight and balance calculations, and compliance with hazardous materials regulations for air transport.

Emergency Procedures:

- The certificate may require operators to have documented emergency procedures in place for addressing in-flight emergencies, cargo-related incidents, or other safety incidents involving cargo aircraft.

Environmental Compliance:

- Some certificates may consider environmental factors, such as noise pollution and emissions control, especially for cargo aircraft operating in and around airports.

Validity and Renewal:

- Air Cargo Maintenance Certificates typically have a validity period, after which the aircraft must undergo another round of inspections and maintenance to renew the certificate.

Liability and Insurance:

- Holding a valid certificate can impact insurance coverage, as insurers may consider it a positive factor when providing coverage for potential cargo aircraft-related incidents.

Regulatory Compliance:

- These certificates are essential to demonstrate compliance with aviation regulations and safety standards established by national and international aviation authorities, including the Federal Aviation Administration (FAA) in the United States and the European Union Aviation Safety Agency (EASA) in

Europe.

In summary, an Air Cargo Maintenance Certificate is a critical document that ensures the safe and reliable operation of cargo aircraft in the transportation of air cargo. It plays a vital role in aviation safety, regulatory compliance, and the prevention of accidents in air cargo transportation.

Cargo ships sea worthiness certificate

A Cargo Ship Sea Worthiness Certificate, also known as a Certificate of Sea Worthiness, is an official document that attests to the seaworthiness and fitness for sailing of a cargo ship. This certificate is a crucial part of maritime safety and is typically issued by maritime authorities or classification societies. Here are key points about the Cargo Ship Sea Worthiness Certificate:

Purpose:

- The primary purpose of a Cargo Ship Sea Worthiness Certificate is to confirm that a cargo ship is in a condition that allows it to safely navigate and operate in open waters. It is a key document for ensuring maritime safety.

Issuing Authority:

- These certificates are typically issued by recognized maritime authorities or classification societies that have the authority to assess and certify the seaworthiness of ships.

Seaworthiness Assessment:

- To obtain this certificate, a cargo ship must undergo a thorough assessment of its condition, including its hull, machinery, equipment, safety systems, and navigation instruments. This assessment verifies that the ship meets international safety standards and regulations.

Regular Inspections:

- Cargo ships are subject to regular inspections to ensure their continued seaworthiness. These inspections may include annual surveys, special surveys, and intermediate surveys, depending on the ship's age and usage.

Safety Equipment and Systems:

- The certificate confirms that the cargo ship is equipped with the necessary safety equipment and systems, such as lifeboats, fire-fighting equipment, navigation lights, and communication systems, to ensure the safety of the crew, cargo, and the ship itself.

Hull Integrity:

- The certificate verifies the structural integrity of the ship's hull, ensuring that it can withstand the stresses and conditions of the open sea.

Operational Capability:

- It confirms that the ship's propulsion systems, including engines and steering mechanisms, are in good working order and capable of safe operation.

Navigation Equipment:

- Cargo ships must have operational navigation and communication equipment to ensure safe navigation and the ability to communicate with other vessels and shore authorities.

Cargo Handling Systems:

- If applicable, the certificate may assess the cargo handling systems, ensuring that they are suitable for the types of cargo the ship is intended to carry.

Environmental Compliance:

- Some certificates may consider environmental factors, such as compliance with international regulations related to ballast water management and emissions control.

Liability and Insurance:

- Holding a valid Cargo Ship Sea Worthiness Certificate can impact liability and insurance coverage, as it attests to the ship's compliance with safety standards and regulations.

International Recognition:

- These certificates are typically recognized internationally and are essential for cargo ships engaged in international trade and voyages.

Validity and Renewal:

- Cargo Ship Sea Worthiness Certificates have a validity period, and ships must undergo regular surveys and inspections to renew the certificate and maintain their seaworthy status.

In summary, a Cargo Ship Sea Worthiness Certificate is a critical document that ensures the safe operation of cargo ships and compliance with international maritime safety standards. It plays a vital role in maritime safety, regulatory compliance, and the prevention of accidents at sea.

Staffs health regulation

Staff Health Regulations refer to a set of rules, guidelines, and measures established by employers, regulatory authorities, or public health agencies to safeguard the health and well-being of employees in the workplace. These regulations aim to create a safe and healthy work environment, prevent the spread of infectious diseases, and promote the overall welfare of workers. Here are key points about staff health regulations:

Purpose:

- The primary purpose of staff health regulations is to protect the physical and mental health of employees while they are at work. This includes preventing workplace injuries, occupational illnesses, and exposure to health hazards.

Compliance and Legal Framework:

- Staff health regulations are often established within a legal framework and must be followed by employers to ensure compliance with labor laws and occupational health and safety regulations.

Key Components:

- Staff health regulations typically cover various aspects, including workplace safety, sanitation, hygiene, health surveillance, vaccination requirements, first aid, and emergency response procedures.

Health and Safety Policies:

- Employers are often required to develop and implement health and safety policies that outline their commitment to creating a safe workplace and complying with relevant regulations.

Workplace Safety:

- Regulations may require employers to assess workplace hazards, implement safety measures, provide protective equipment, and conduct regular safety training for employees.

Sanitation and Hygiene:

- Employers must maintain clean and hygienic workplaces, including restroom facilities, break areas, and eating areas. Handwashing facilities and hygiene practices are often emphasized.

Health Surveillance:

- Some industries and occupations may require regular health assessments and medical examinations for employees to monitor their well-being and detect any occupational health issues.

Vaccination Requirements:

- In certain workplaces, such as healthcare facilities, employees may be required to receive vaccinations to prevent the spread of contagious diseases, such as influenza or COVID-19.

First Aid:

- Employers are typically required to provide first aid facilities, supplies, and trained personnel to respond to workplace injuries or medical emergencies.

Emergency Response:

- Regulations may outline procedures for responding to workplace accidents, fires, chemical spills, or other emergencies, ensuring the safety of employees during such events.

Mental Health:

- Modern staff health regulations increasingly address mental health concerns in the workplace, including stress management, harassment prevention, and providing access to mental health support services.

Training and Education:

- Employers often have a responsibility to educate employees about workplace health and safety regulations, potential hazards, and safe work practices.

Documentation and Reporting:

- Compliance with staff health regulations may require maintaining records of workplace incidents, injuries, illnesses, and safety inspections. Reporting requirements to regulatory authorities may also exist.

Enforcement and Penalties:

- Regulatory authorities or government agencies responsible for labor and health and safety enforcement may impose penalties on employers who fail to comply with staff health regulations.

In summary, staff health regulations are a vital component of ensuring the well-being of employees in the workplace. They cover a wide range of health and safety aspects, with the goal of preventing accidents, injuries, and illnesses and promoting a healthy work environment. Compliance with these regulations is essential for both employers and employees to create and maintain safe and productive workplaces.

Up keeping of premises certificate

An "Upkeeping of Premises Certificate" refers to an official document or certification that is issued to confirm that a property or premises is being adequately maintained, both in terms of cleanliness and safety. This certificate is typically issued by relevant authorities or regulatory agencies to ensure that property owners or managers are meeting specific maintenance and safety standards. Here are key points about the "Upkeeping of Premises Certificate":

Purpose:

- The primary purpose of an Upkeeping of Premises Certificate is to verify that a property or premises is being maintained in a manner that ensures the safety and well-being of occupants and visitors.

Issuing Authority:

- These certificates are usually issued by local government

authorities, building departments, or health and safety agencies responsible for regulating property maintenance and safety standards.

Maintenance Standards:

- The certificate is issued based on compliance with specific maintenance and safety standards, which may include cleanliness, structural integrity, fire safety, sanitation, and other factors depending on the type of premises.

Regular Inspections:

- Premises that require this certificate are often subject to regular inspections by authorized inspectors to ensure that they meet the established maintenance and safety standards.

Cleanliness and Hygiene:

- The certificate typically confirms that the premises are clean, well-kept, and free from health hazards. This includes sanitation measures, waste disposal, pest control, and overall cleanliness.

Structural Integrity:

- For buildings and structures, the certificate may verify that the property is structurally sound, with no imminent risk of collapse or unsafe conditions.

Fire Safety:

- Fire safety standards are essential for premises with occupancies. The certificate may confirm that fire safety equipment is in place and functional, and that escape routes are clear and well-marked.

Health and Safety Measures:

- Depending on the nature of the premises (e.g., residential, commercial, industrial), specific health and safety measures may be assessed. For example, restaurants may need to comply with food safety regulations.

Validity and Renewal:

- The Upkeeping of Premises Certificate is typically issued for a specified period (e.g., annually) and must be renewed after each period to ensure ongoing compliance.

Liability and Compliance:

- Property owners or managers are responsible for maintaining their premises in compliance with relevant regulations. Holding a valid certificate demonstrates compliance with maintenance and safety standards.

Penalties for Non-Compliance:

- Failure to maintain premises in accordance with established standards and obtain the required certificate may result in penalties, fines, or legal action by regulatory authorities.

Public Assurance:

- For properties open to the public, such as restaurants, hotels, and entertainment venues, having an Upkeeping of Premises Certificate can provide assurance to customers and visitors that the property is safe and well-maintained.

In summary, an Upkeeping of Premises Certificate is a vital document that confirms the proper maintenance and safety of a property or premises. It ensures that the property meets established standards, promotes safety, and protects the health and well-being of occupants and visitors. Compliance with these regulations and obtaining the certificate is crucial for property owners and managers to operate safely and legally.

Routine maintenance of building records and Dos and Donts while handling different documents.

Routine Maintenance of Building Records: Routine maintenance of building records is essential to ensure the proper management and upkeep of a property. It involves systematically documenting and updating information related to the building's construction, maintenance, and safety. Here are key points regarding the routine maintenance of building records:

1. **Documentation:** Maintain organized records in both physical and digital formats. Common categories of records include architectural plans, maintenance logs, inspection reports, warranties, and permits.

2. **Maintenance Logs:** Keep detailed maintenance logs that record when maintenance activities were performed, what was done, and by whom. This helps track the history of repairs and maintenance.

3. **Inspection Reports:** Regularly inspect the building for safety and maintenance issues. Document these inspections, noting any concerns or actions taken to address them.

4. Legal Documents: Keep copies of all relevant legal documents, such as property deeds, leases, zoning permits, and licenses, in a secure location.

5. Safety Documentation: Maintain records of safety measures, including fire safety inspections, emergency evacuation plans, and safety equipment inspections. Ensure compliance with safety regulations.

6. Contracts and Agreements: Keep copies of contracts with service providers, including maintenance contractors, security services, and utility providers. Ensure that contracts are up to date and renew them as necessary.

7. Financial Records: Track expenses related to building maintenance and repairs, including invoices, receipts, and payment records. This aids in budgeting and financial planning.

8. Warranty Information: Document warranties for building components and equipment. Include details such as warranty start and end dates, terms, and contact information for warranty providers.

9. Energy Usage Data: Maintain records of energy consumption and utility bills. Monitoring energy usage can help identify opportunities for energy efficiency improvements.

10. Building Plans: Keep copies of architectural and engineering plans, including blueprints, electrical diagrams, and plumbing layouts. These documents are crucial for renovations or modifications.

11. Permits and Approvals: Maintain records of permits obtained for construction or renovations. Ensure compliance with local building codes and regulations.

12. Accessibility Records: If applicable, document accessibility measures to comply with disability access regulations, including ramp installations, elevator maintenance, and accessible restroom facilities.

13. Training Records: Keep records of employee training related to building safety, emergency procedures, and equipment operation. Ensure that employees are adequately trained.

14. Disaster Preparedness: Create and maintain disaster preparedness plans, including records of drills and emergency response procedures.

15. Data Security: Protect digital records with secure backup systems and cybersecurity measures. Maintain physical records in a secure and climate-controlled environment.

Dos and Don'ts While Handling Different Documents: When handling various types of documents, it's important to follow best practices to ensure their integrity, confidentiality, and accessibility. Here are some dos and don'ts for managing documents:

Dos:

1. **Organize:** Maintain a well-organized filing system to facilitate document retrieval.
2. **Label:** Clearly label documents with relevant information, including dates, titles, and document types.
3. **Secure:** Protect sensitive documents with secure storage and access controls.
4. **Backup:** Regularly back up digital documents to prevent data loss.
5. **Shred:** Properly dispose of sensitive documents by shredding them to protect against identity theft.
6. **Train:** Train employees on document management procedures and security protocols.
7. **Review:** Periodically review and update document retention policies to ensure compliance with legal requirements.
8. **Audit:** Conduct document audits to verify the accuracy and completeness of records.

Don'ts:

1. **Don't Ignore Security:** Neglecting document security can lead to data breaches and privacy violations.
2. **Don't Overretain:** Avoid retaining unnecessary documents beyond their required retention periods, as this can lead to clutter and increased risk.
3. **Don't Share Without Authorization:** Do not share sensitive documents with unauthorized individuals.
4. **Don't Use Weak Passwords:** Use strong, unique passwords to protect digital documents from unauthorized access.
5. **Don't Mix Personal and Business Documents:** Keep personal and business documents separate to maintain privacy and clarity.
6. **Don't Delay Recordkeeping:** Timely recordkeeping helps prevent document loss and ensures accurate information.
7. **Don't Ignore Compliance:** Failure to comply with legal document retention requirements can lead to legal consequences.

Effective document management and routine maintenance of building records are essential for organizations to operate efficiently, maintain compliance, and safeguard important information.

THE END

Did you love *Procedure and Documentation in Supply Chain Management*? Then you should read *Port Terminals System - Conveyor and Equipment Maintenance*[1] by SANJIVAN SAINI!

[2]

"Port Terminals System - Conveyor and Equipment Maintenance" provides acomprehensive guide to the maintenance practices and techniques required for efficient operation of conveyors and equipment in port terminals. This book is designed to assist port professionals, maintenance personnel, and logistics professionals in understanding the principles and best practices of conveyor and equipment maintenance in the context of port operations.

"Port Terminals System - Conveyor and Equipment Maintenance" is a vital resource that equips professionals with the knowledge and tools needed to maintain the lifeline of port terminals. Sanjivan Saini's

1. https://books2read.com/u/bQe7Ve

2. https://books2read.com/u/bQe7Ve

expertise and dedication to excellence shine through every page, making this book an invaluable asset in the world of logistics and transportation. Whether you're an industry veteran or a newcomer, this book will empower you to meet the challenges of maintaining port terminal systems head-on, ultimately leading to smoother operations, reduced downtime, and increased profitability.**1. Terminal operation2. Material Handling Equipment3. Container Yard4. Conveyors5. Transportation – Informations**The book concludes by emphasizing the importance of regular maintenance and adopting advanced technologies for efficient and reliable conveyor and equipment operation in port terminals. It highlights the significance of safety practices, documentation, and continuous improvementin maintenance processes. By following the principles and guidelines outlined in this book, port professionals and maintenance personnel can enhance the performance, longevity, and safety of conveyor systems and equipment in port terminals. In the fast-paced world of global trade and commerce, the efficiency of port terminals plays a pivotal role in ensuring the smooth flow of goods and maintaining economic stability.

"Port Terminals System - Conveyor and Equipment Maintenance" by Sanjivan Saini is a comprehensive guide that unveils the criticalaspects of managing and maintaining the heart of any port terminal - its conveyor and equipment systems. As a seasoned expert with decades of experience in the field, Sanjivan Saini brings a wealth of knowledge and practical insights to this essential reference book. Port terminals, with their complex machinery and highdemand operations, require meticulous maintenance to minimize downtime, ensure safety, and maximize productivity. This book serves as an indispensable resource for port terminal managers, maintenance personnel, engineers, and anyone involved in the logistics and transportation industry

www.ingramcontent.com/pod-product-compliance
Lightning Source LLC
LaVergne TN
LVHW022043200926
848481LV00003B/763